autoreduction

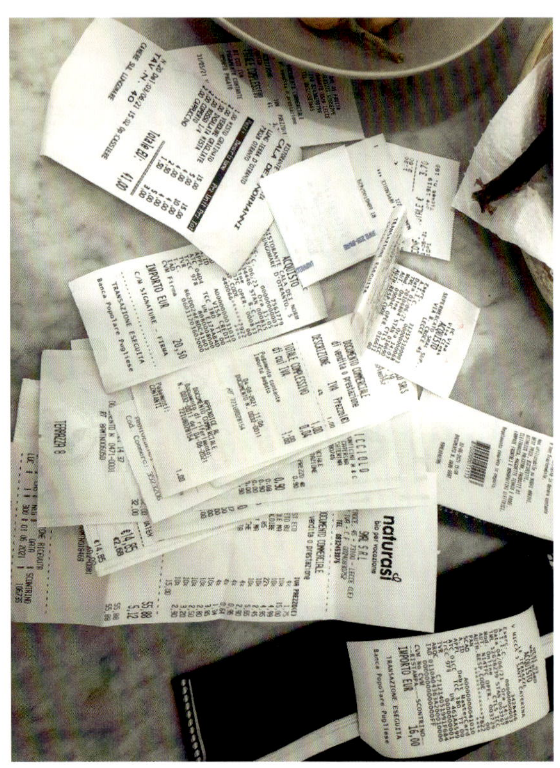

Mousse Publishing — Progetto — Oaza Books

autoreduction

Noah Barker
Dora Budor
Niloufar Emamifar
Stefano Faoro
Michèle Graf and Selina Grüter
Ser Serpas
Marina Vishmidt

edited by Dora Budor

Contents

A Case of Enrichment

Noah Barker

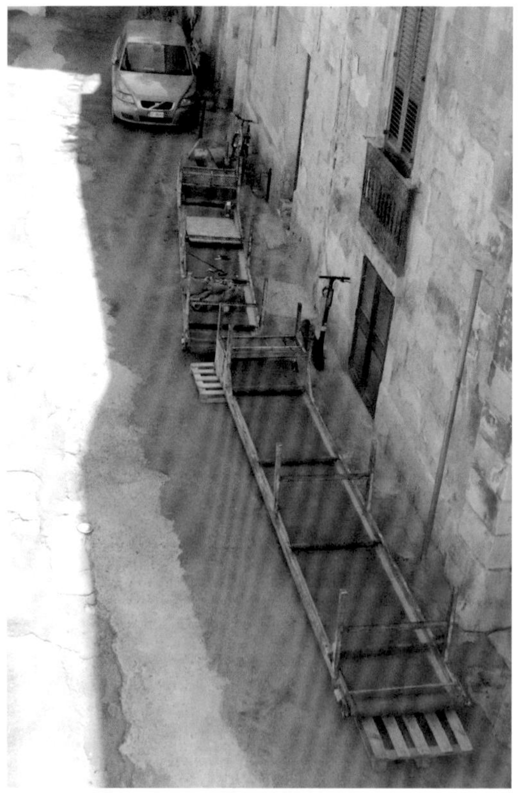

Progetto occupies a palazzo in Lecce, the capital of an eponymous Italian province famous now for its coast but once for its nicotine. In this way, it was and remains a region central to the psychic economy of the republic: snuff-inhaling Milanese industrialists were quite literally addicted to the Mezzogiorno's agricultural exploits. For two centuries, in field and factory, most such workers were women known as *tabacchine*. Employed as the cheapest available labor, their exploitation exceeded the wage: as the conveyor belt "marched," they would sing songs about being forced to parade for Il Duce in the provincial capital.[1] In July 2021, Dora Budor initiated the relocation of conveyor tables from a tobacco factory where they had sat decommissioned for three decades to Progetto's exhibition rooms. The chambers scaled for lavish living struggled to contain the six-meter spans of steel in a gesture that grafted together axes of production and reproduction, accumulation and expenditure.

In October 2021, the tables were renovated for dining at an *agriturismo* hotel opened by the inheritor of the former factory from which they had originally come. Put back into service, they told a story about something formerly viewed as detritus, with the tables elevated to the center of the local economy in a new way. Sociologists Luc Boltanski and Arnaud Esquerre have recently studied the ways in which objects, places, and experiences undergo such transformations in what they call the *enrichment economy*.[2] An essential feature of the enrichment economy is the valorizing of the past in fabricated and rehearsed narratives that sanitize and streamline historical consciousness, just as the tables do. In the wake of an economic crisis beginning in the mid-1960s attributed to surplus productive capacity, the Western centralization of capital was maintained by delocalizing production. In the province of Lecce, the decline of the tobacco industry, in part due to European Union restrictions on state monopoly and in part to its eventual sale to Philip Morris, has led to the all-too-familiar effect of deindustrialization and one of the highest unemployment rates in the EU. The enrichment economy responds by emphasizing formally marginal forms of wealth creation, namely tourism and the sale of luxury goods, that operate not by exporting commodities but by importing more affluent, less locally rooted consumers.

The boom mentality pervading the still-underexploited real-estate market in Lecce causes one to overhear pronouncements in the region such as, "It's like Tuscany in the '70s." Indeed, a first-time visitor boasted of buying a palazzo straight off the plane: €500,000 for more rooms than you can count. Boltanski and Esquerre turn to the firsthand account of a secondhand dealer in order to outline the ways consumers have taken on the mind of merchants, whereby the goal is to "get a break"—that is, to come across a secondhand object that can be sold for an amount much higher than the purchase price. To succeed, dealers have to avoid antique shops and salons where "the merchandise has already been picked over"; rather, they need to "be present at the moment of unpacking where the unsorted contents of cleared-out houses, apartments, basements, or attics arrive directly."[3] In the shops of Puglia, the unpacking is happening now. The things a merchant buys and sells are transformed from mere ends in themselves into commodities through the currently raging cycle of exchange in pursuit of increased money, according to Marx's famous formulation M-C-M'.

In turn, the commodity is universalized in its exchange by means of the common placeholder of money. This universality insinuates a freedom for the market as well as liberation for the circulating objects, achieving the dream of liberal economic thought in the Enlightenment. It wouldn't be until the appearance of the standard form of the mass-produced commodity, however, that the advantages of this ideology could deliver on the hypotheses of *anyone buying anything anywhere* to emerge, and with it an anonymity of consumption. A Cartesian market space then superseded what had been "a set of points equipped with differential properties" in which profit had been previously garnered through the exploitation of distance.[4] The relations of anonymous exchange are legislated by the legally binding language of institutions. In the exhibition at Progetto, in the rooms of the palazzo, two poems qua artworks by Michèle Graf and Selina Grüter appeared in English and Italian. Purchases compose their readymade diction; receipts cut and pasted convey a ransom note's sense of anonymity. In the duo's *Pocket Liners* series (2021), the edge of each word excerpted from separate transactions calls to mind the blade that spliced them, as if holding the viewer captive. The producer of artworks, shown to be a consumer of commodities, is doubly beholden to the language of the market for the wares they must not only create but also sell.

The mass production of commodities assumes the mass production of trash, as M-C-M' requires the "valorization of the differences always purporting to be new" in its cycles of transaction. Ser Serpas's works at Progetto foregrounded their common compositional materials as garbage against the particularities of the objects themselves. In roofless rooms atop the palazzo, roadside debris sourced between Salento's villages formed sculptures assembled with minimal manipulation of the original objects. A few moments of spirited play in the patinaed bricolages, however, made for photogenic compositions against the stone walls and seductive open sky. They furnished the ruinous rooms with spontaneous poesis of the sort that litters our mind in Instagram posts of the universalized aesthetician. Aside from documenting the temporary arrangements for likes, the collector is left to nominate the work for permanent preservation, preventing the return of materials to the streets. Boltanski and Esquerre turn to Michael Thompson's *Rubbish Theory* (1979) to describe how "things at the heart of the enrichment economy may have long been treated as trash," in contrast with industrially produced goods, in that the most pertinent items in the enrichment economy see their prices to go up over time.

The collector is the preeminent merchantilized consumer, seeking an advantageous price for pleasure gained in the rub of distinction, a practice that involves bringing together different objects of a similar order for setting apart the self. Boltanski and Esquerre assess collecting as a form of attributing value that "helped shift the modalities of wealth creation when, as the production of standard objects was increasingly outsourced to low-wage countries, the dynamics of capitalism turned much more strongly toward exploitation of the past."[5] The collector is of course a significant participant in the art system, one who was particularly present in Lecce during the run of *Autoreduction* due to a boutique art fair, Palai, that opened concurrently with the exhibition. (The pairing occurred again in 2022 when Palai coincided with a project by Stefano Faoro, *U.S. Go Home*.)[6] The combination of art collectors, tourism, and cultural heritage has recently been the focus of Italy's leading galleries in the founding of a consortium, Italics: Art and Landscape, to promote destinations across Italy. Aside from its Instagram presence, the consortium organizes an annual weekend-long exhibition, Panorama. Its first iteration was held in conjunction with the Italian government's City of Culture program on the island of Procida, while the second, occurring in 2022, is to be held in Monopoli, a coastal town in the province of Lecce. Where the land meets the sea, fortifications make for spectacular backdrops, and the defensive positions of the past open themselves to visitors who seek a juxtaposition of art's internal difference, always slightly the same, with distinct local heritage.

Perhaps a waterfront town isn't such a surprising location for luxury to situate itself. A more jarring transformation of a site, mentioned by Boltanski and Esquerre at the start of their book *Enrichment*, is what occurred at the former FIAT factory in Turin. It now houses shops, a hotel, and Pinacoteca Agnelli, the art collection of the company's former CEO. It's made an all-the-more potent crystallization of the churning operations of the economy when the authors follow historical sociologist Giovanni Arrighi in stressing "the intensification of conflicts between labor and capital from the late 1960s to the mid-1970s," clashes that "were particularly pronounced in Europe, especially in France and Italy, where they marked the exhaustion of 'Fordian' arrangements."[7] Such arrangements involved the Communist Party's complicity in increased productivity's being contingent on a rising standard of living while its sole weapon was the strike. Eventually the complicity of the party was contested, and the factory as the traditional site of struggle was abandoned in favor of the tactic of *autoriduzione*. Resistance occurred in consumption rather than production, by not paying full price for goods and services in order to counter price increases. The strategy, which was first practiced in response to rises in bus fare by FIAT workers employed at the very plant that now houses art, lends its anglicization, *autoreduction*, as the title of this volume, and the exhibition it commemorates.

1 *On the 19th of April*
Came the Inspector
With a request that the lady workers put on a parade

All the girls
Said they weren't having it
"We won't find husbands there!"

And so the Inspector
Said he wouldn't tolerate their attitude
"If you don't come to Lecce, I won't let you sign in anymore"...

When we arrive in Lecce
Those dim-witted Lecce boys
Say "Aren't they pretty"

This song is included in Fabiola Pesare, "Women in the Economy of the Salento: Tobacco and Tobacco Workers in the Province of Lecce," in *The Language of the Mother in History: New Cultural Itineraries*, ed. Anna Trono, K. Rizzello, and F. Ruppi (Lecce, Italy: Del Grifo Ed., 2008), 395.

2 Luc Boltanski and Arnaud Esquerre, *Enrichment: A Critique of Commodities*, trans. Catherine Porter (Cambridge: Polity Press, 2020).

3 Ibid., 28.

4 Ibid., 184.

5 Ibid., 200.

6 The project by Faoro was also hosted by Progetto, presented in a storefront space of the building not previously used for exhibitions. While occurring separately from *Autoreduction*, it has been reconstituted in this volume.

7 Ibid., 80.

Banquet

Dora Budor

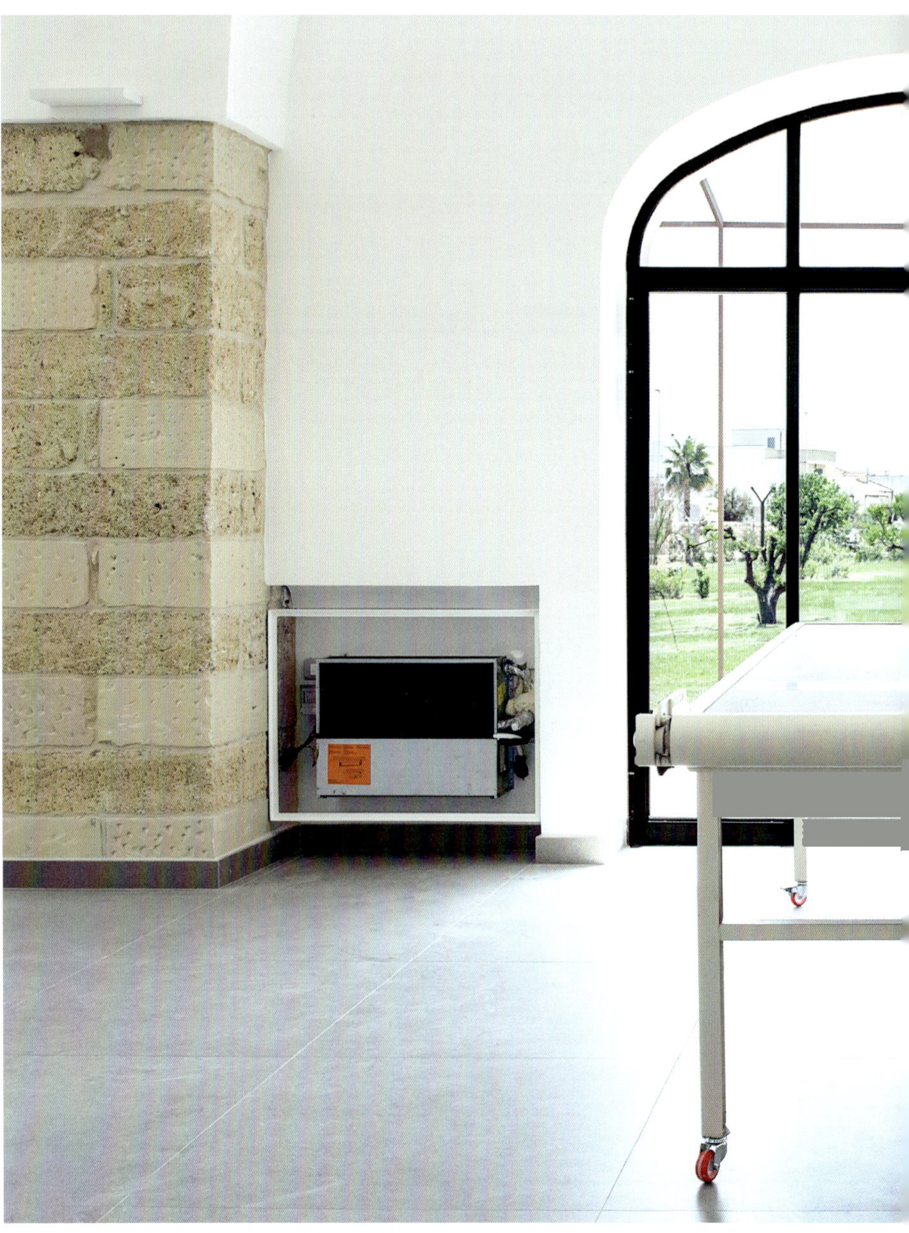

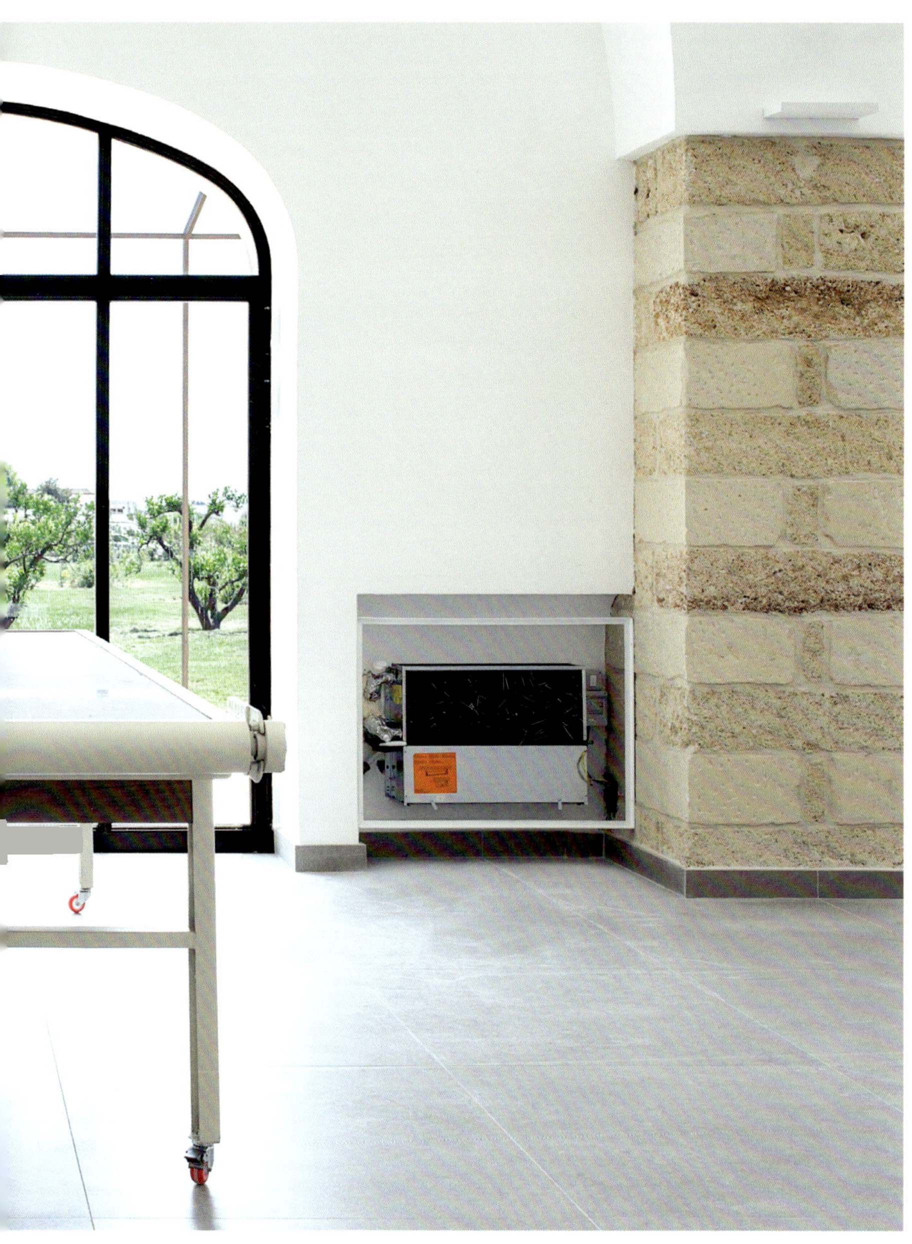

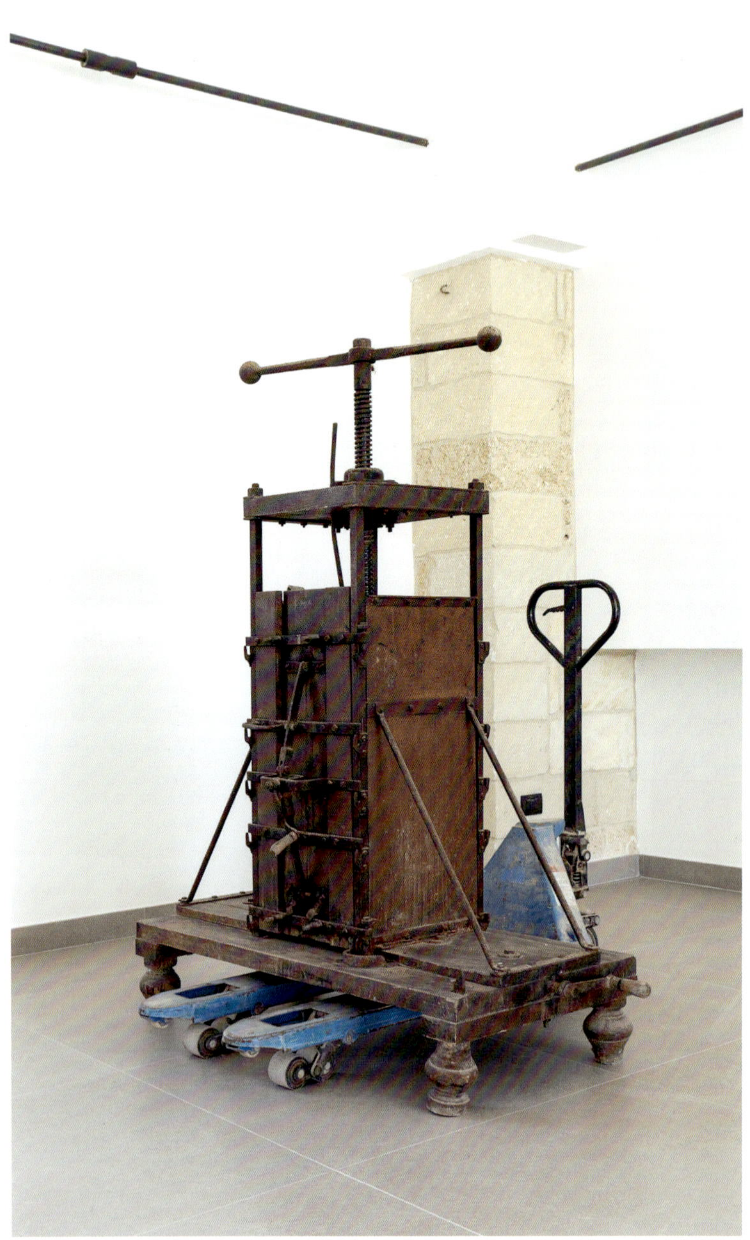

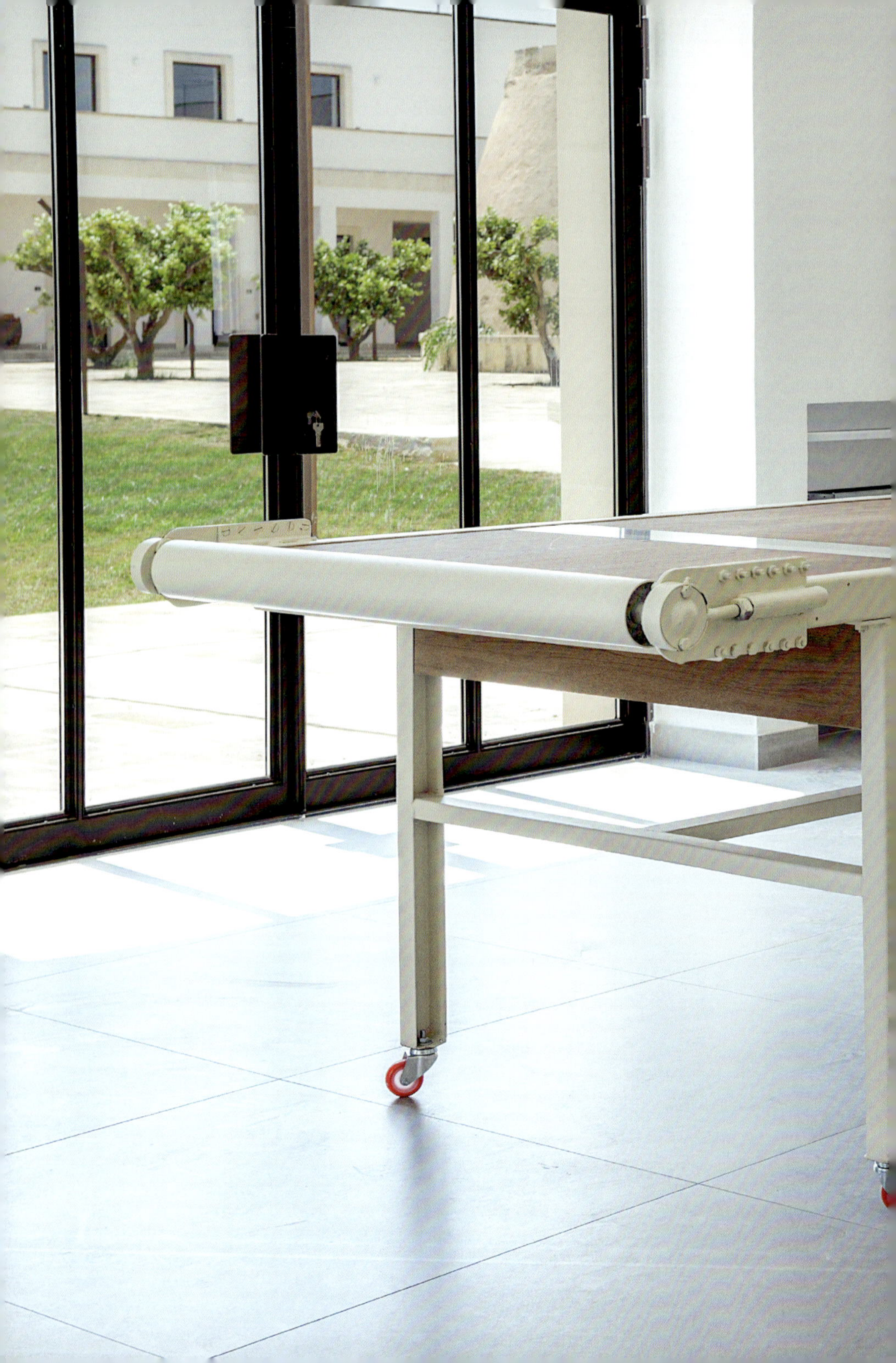

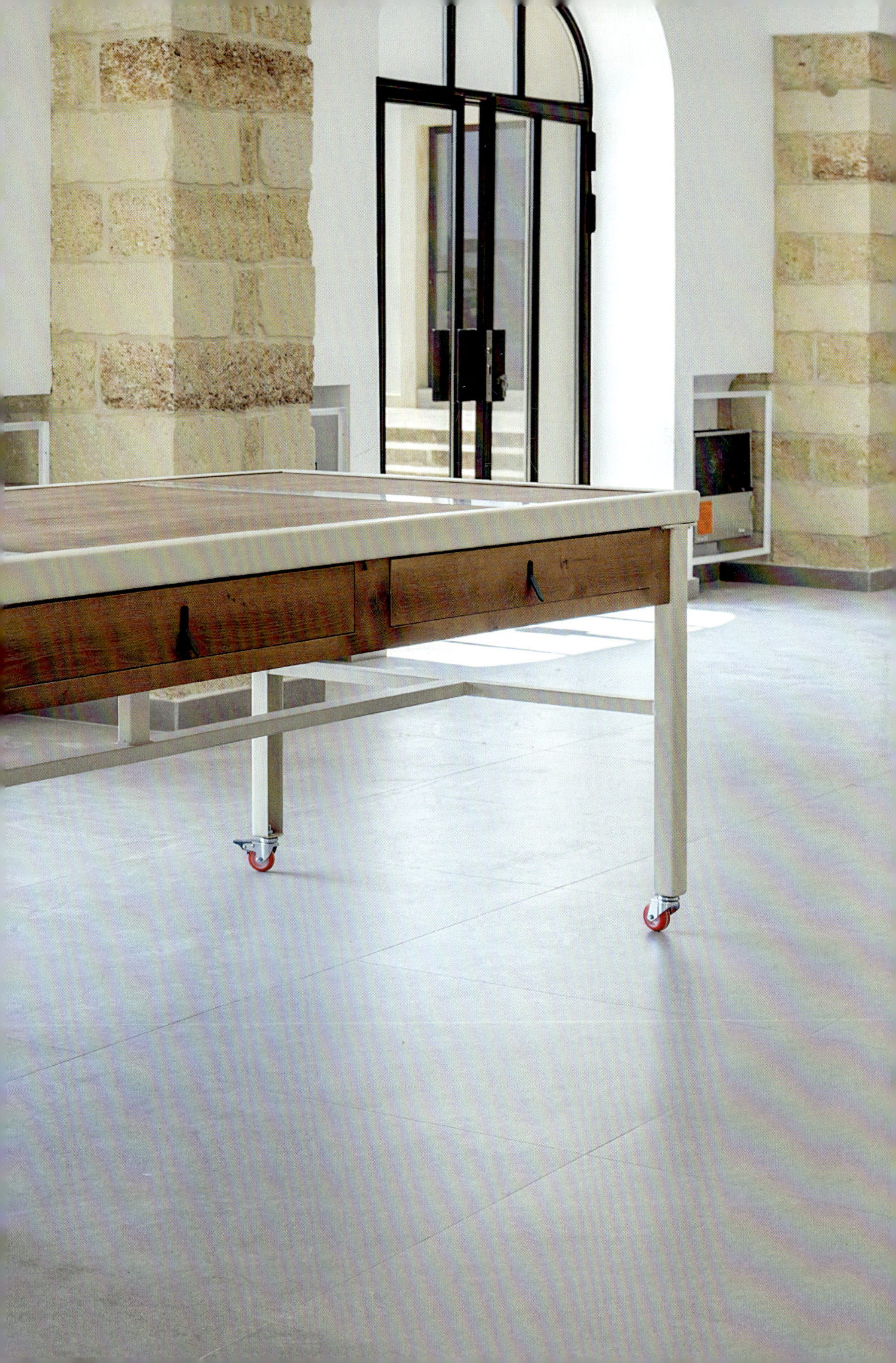

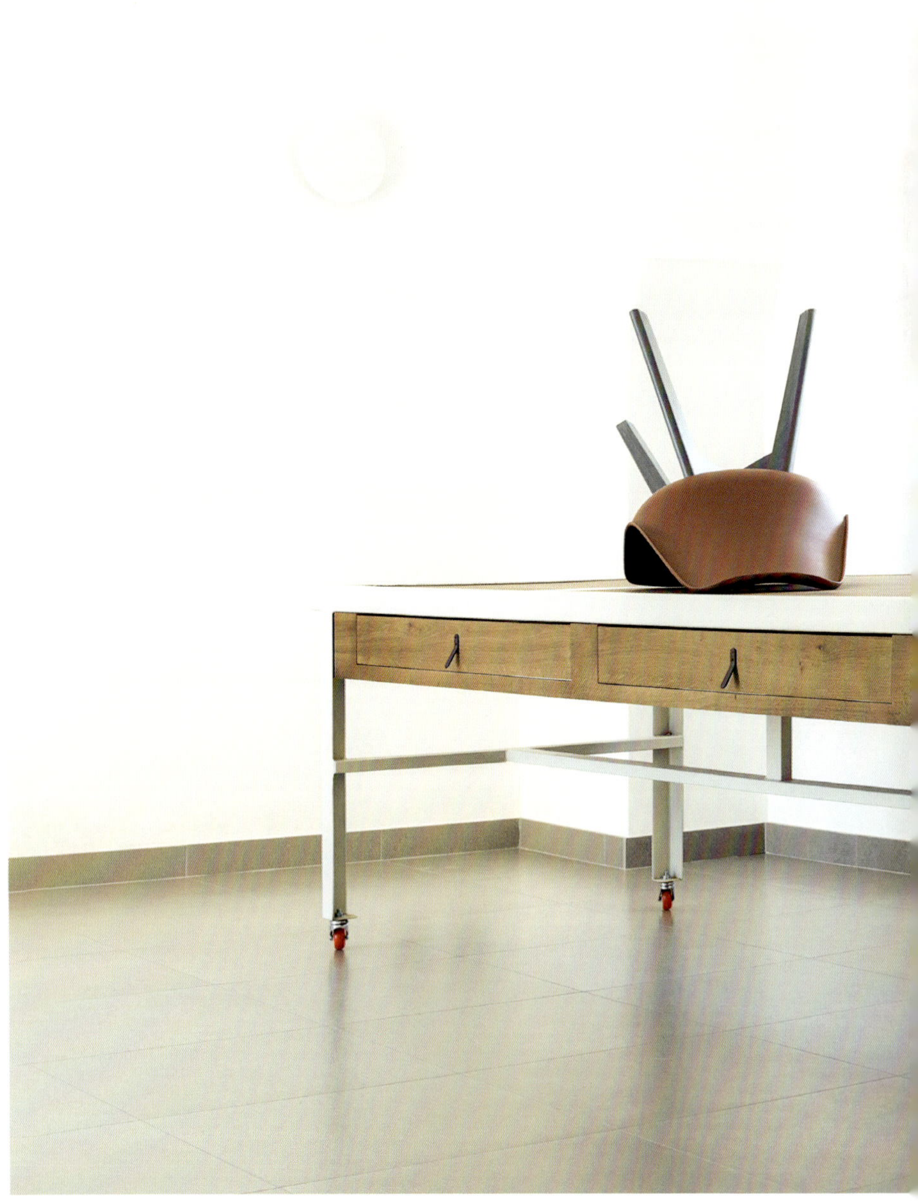

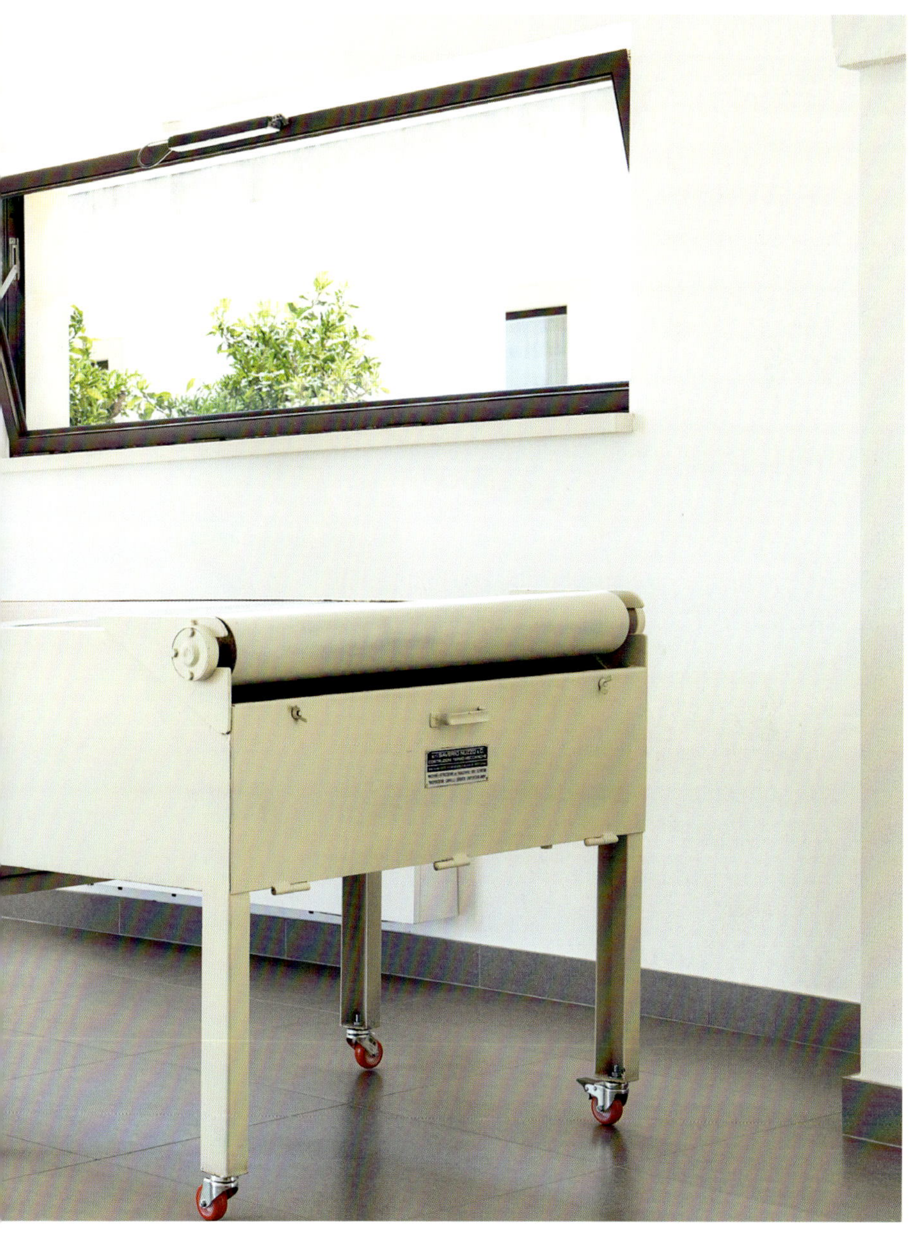

Isn't Anything

Ser Serpas

embarrassing storing around within roads collateral intake grifted
remain in silence
training heavy burgeoning for a chance at good make in time plans
foiled gravitating toward center feeling and folded in it
stargazing matter of fact no coincidences yes and no im the orbital
lesser more and more
a condition of disrepair
dilated figure redacted hippocampus of myrrh
timing killed itself over and over being taking not seeing struggling to
repair and collate the master plan at working to try it out
gravity not telling fielding questions causing a stir at the wrong felt kitchen
tables in set in motion belting they are vibrating coming up on seasons
jealous of the math say i cannot
relate to this and this
slashing the tires healing but cutting broke in touch with you know
the way things flesh out
i tied my intentions very well to a birthright
way of begetting myself i try to laughing at season coastal awareness
not my forte struggling to watch my falling hand yes its an ashtray

soft resounds liquid surrendering founding of transit systems traced back
beyond the pale founding sand in times of willful it beseeched you to
try finding teasing out the calm at most a deaf ambition tracing listicle
generation toppling steeple running along the doubling down on the easy
parts not unintelligible victim sparks tractor beam fungible records of little
talks by the highway praying for side plots what you find and turn away
from such comparisons do more harm than good drop pin the bucket
where one once stood stationary like the way everyone hates the stations
jumped a turnstile bypassed your ennui double embrace i hope for more

illustrious taken aback final abjection in check ways in relating sacrificing
umpire love situation swarm died in lost axis twisted dying in
reveling then found i'm not finding saw see died me fucked
layabout forgiving but not true me and myself traveled well seething
and resolute subject to
umpteenth say me and
object solution my own
way to die forest stain and deserved killing field desert stain maybe the
last instance of anything at all curt but say thank you
maybe

what i did to the rest of them could have been done back and forth
resting over path least resistance is futility moped on anger designing
rage melancholic sonic choices that bleed out, only wish i was conscious
for the beating strategy that would ensue times i was bored and calls
unanswered, slurs midriffs whats taken by surprise really a cadillac for
such desires, please trust me when i say i want you in the worst way

Lecce, June 2021

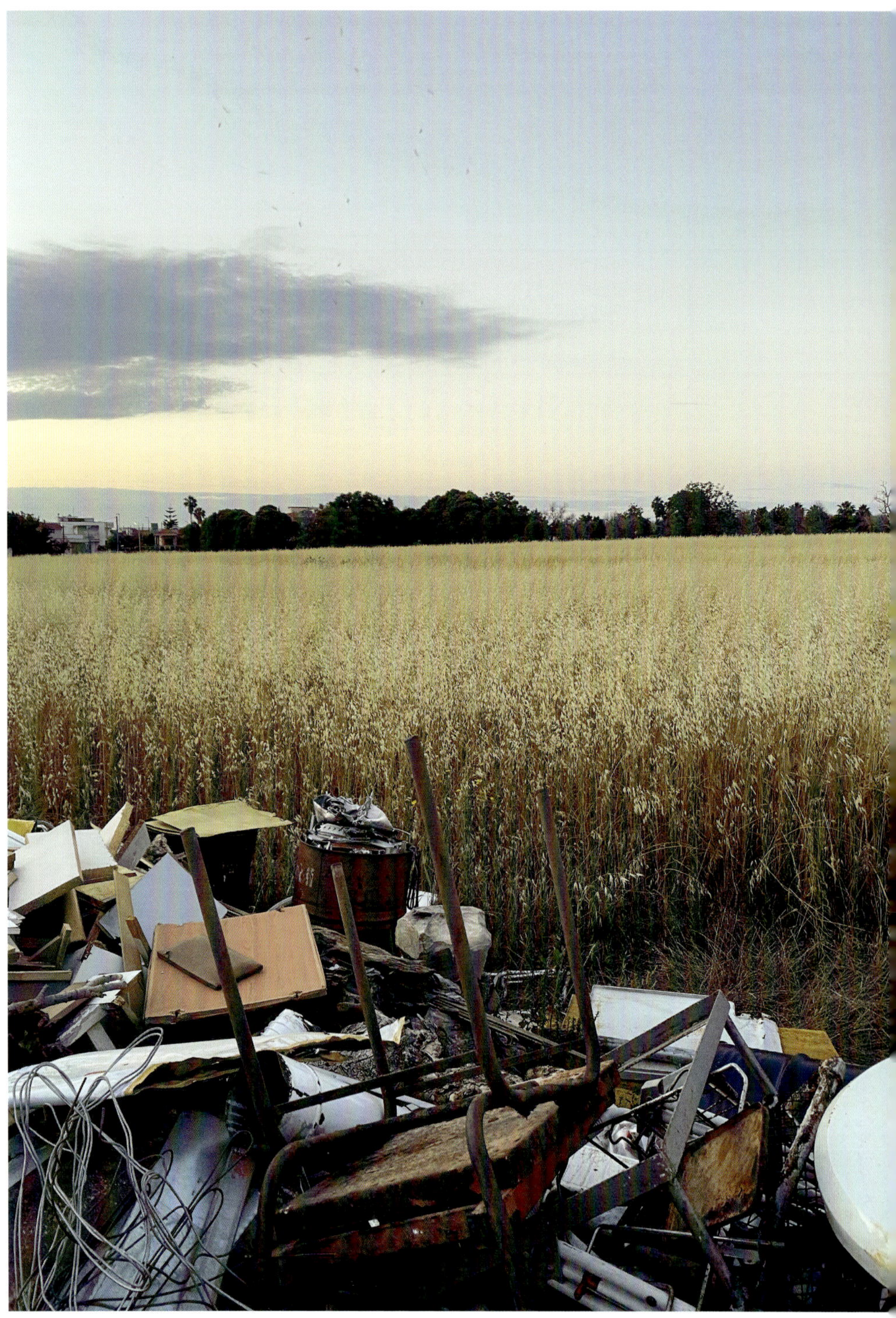

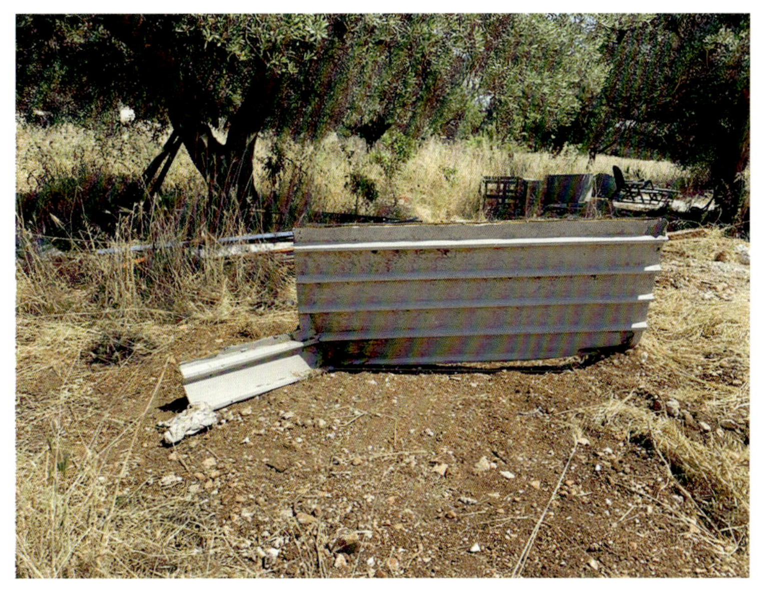

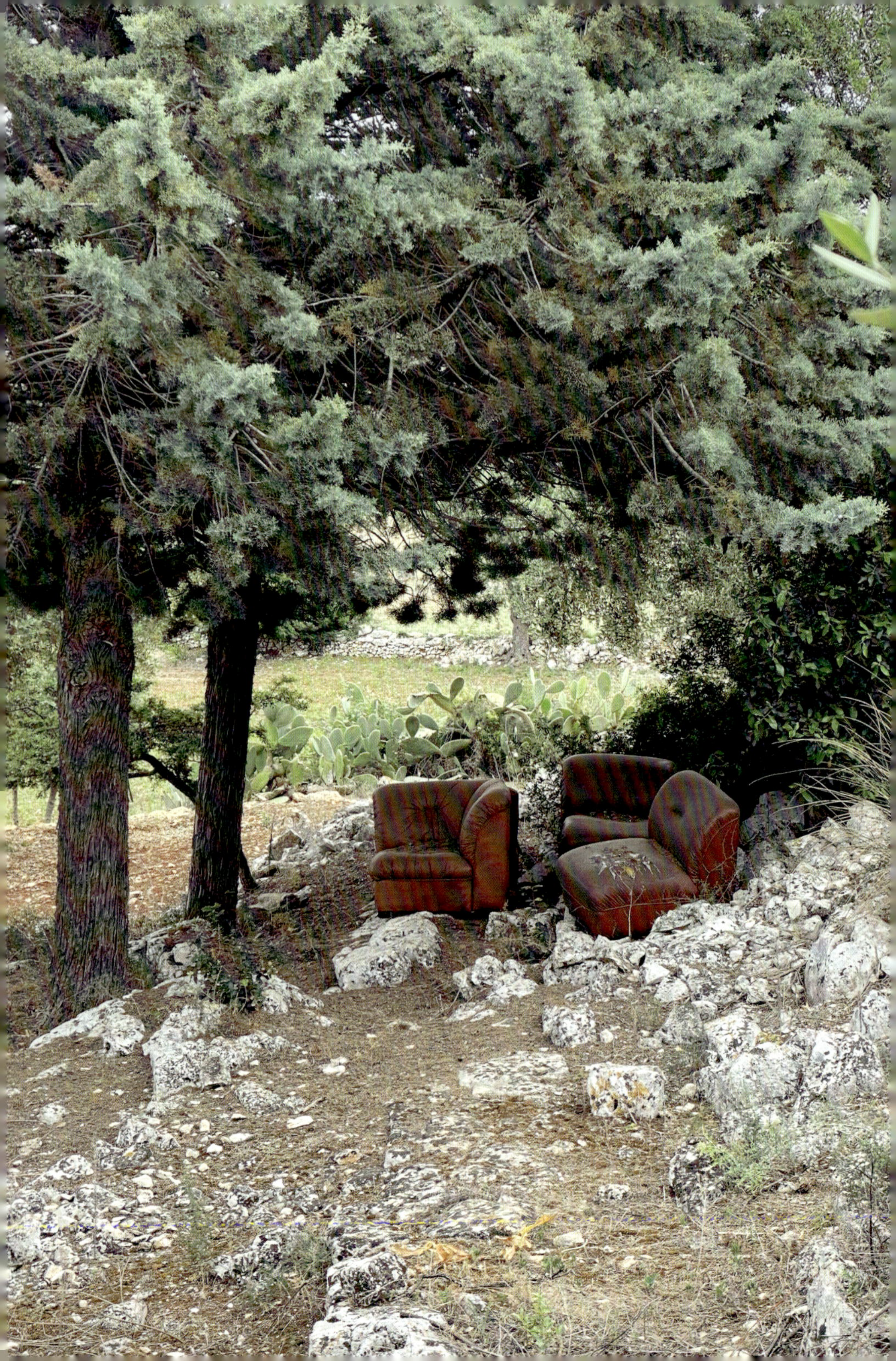

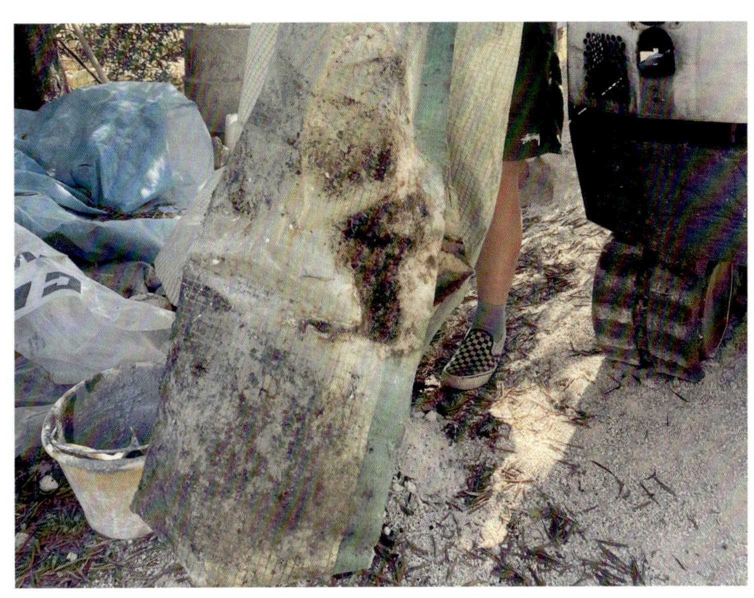

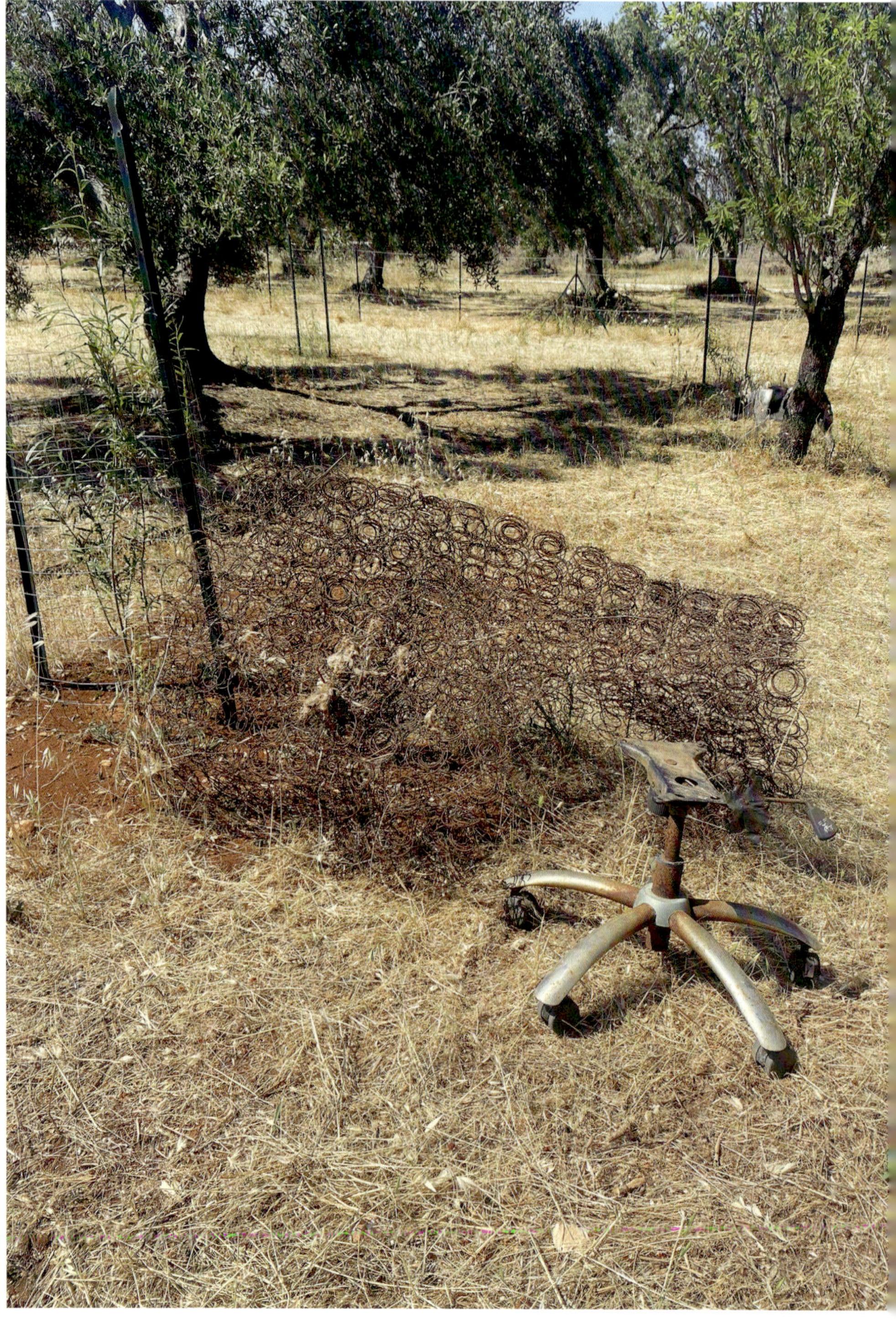

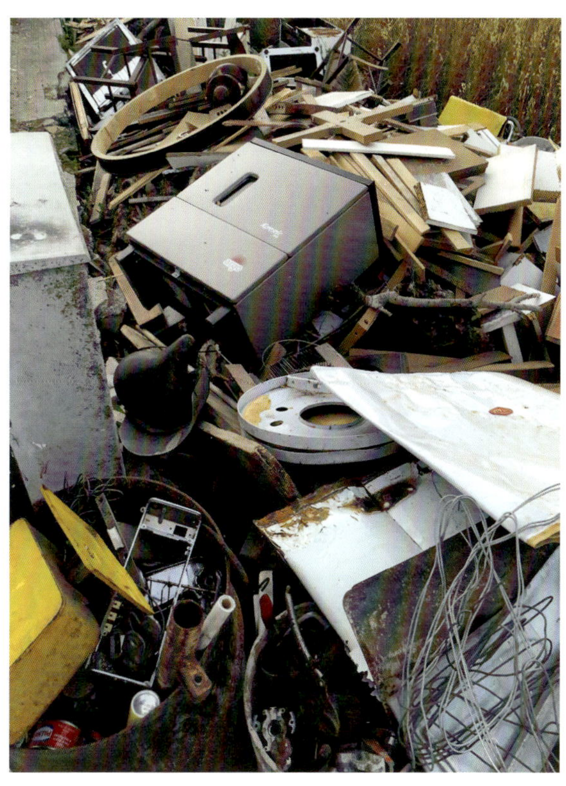

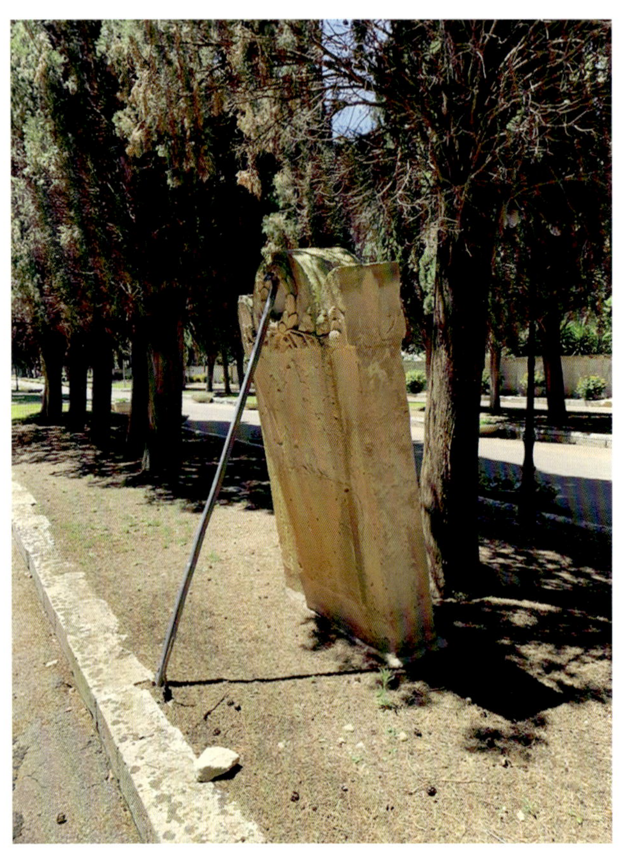

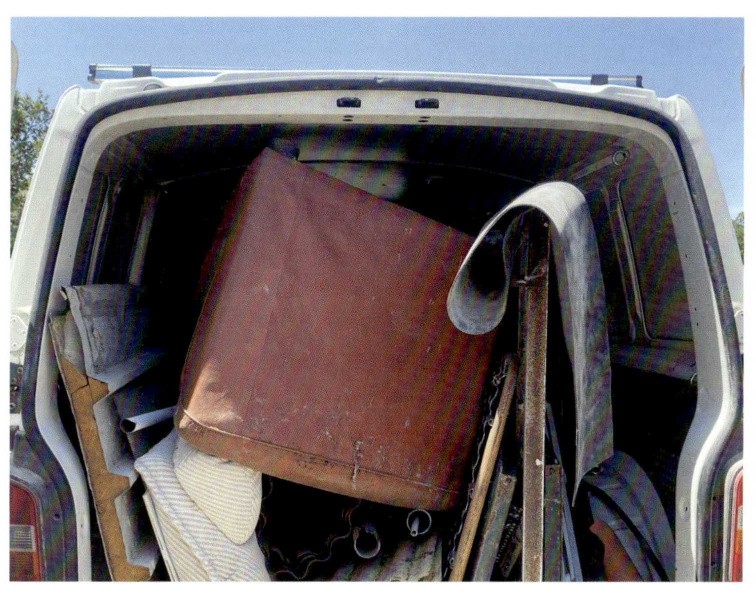

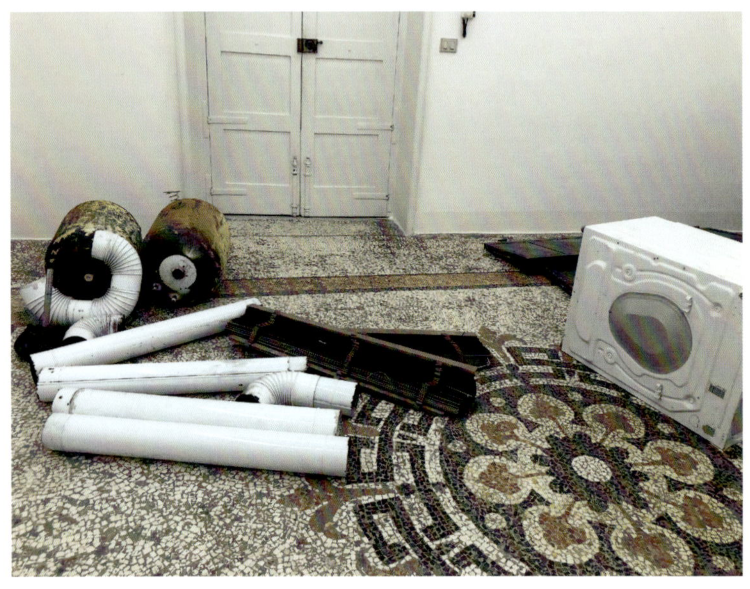

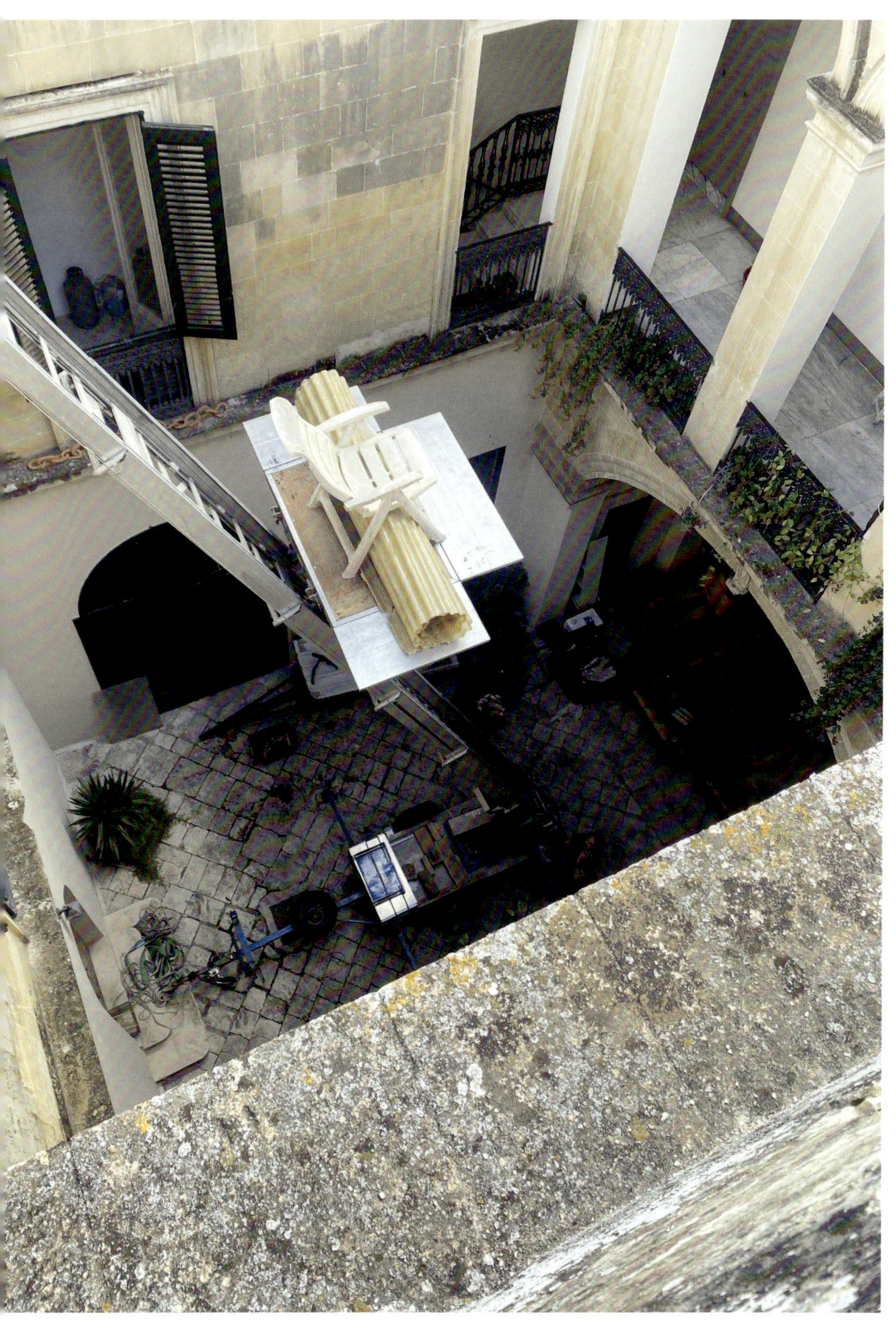

The Besieged Courtyard (Il cortile assediato)

Michèle Graf and Selina Grüter

Giovanna Zangrandi (1910–1988) was an Italian writer born as Alma Bevilacqua in Galliera. She worked in both autobiography and fiction, combining her interest in narrative traditions with her commitment to writing about her experiences as an antifascist resistance fighter. As a courier, she delivered food, arms, and documents to partisan bands in the mountains. After the war, she began writing under the pen name, Giovanna Zangrandi. In her short story "Il cortile assediato" (The Besieged Courtyard), Zangrandi describes her childhood years growing up with socialist parents and the influence of fascist rhetoric she learned at school.

Michèle Graf and Selina Grüter translated "Il cortile assediato" from Italian into English, annotating the work to give context to certain expressions and idioms as well as to emphasize moments of untranslatability.

[...]

A scuola ci andavo alla mattina, in quinta ora, e la consideravo come una necessità un po' stupida, così, tanto per finire. Eravamo una quindicina di ragazze, certune piccoline, timide e insulse, cinque o sei erano grandi, con i seni già fatti dietro la pettorina del grembiule e la crocchia dei capelli con le forcine, due o tre parlavano fitto tra loro schioccando risatine. "Tipi da lasciar perdere" mi aveva detto mia madre e aveva aggiunto secca: "Ti permetto di prendere la bicicletta perché vieni a casa subito, senza far lega e ciarle per via; so io perché. Andare e tornare: capito?".

La bicicletta era una cosa molto importante, eravamo solo in tre a servirci della bicicletta, le altre due stavano lontano sulla riva sinistra del fiume.

Certe volte perfino la maestra mi faceva fare da galoppino con qualche lettera, ci tenevo, la maestra è sempre la maestra.

A questa di quinta però non portavo particolare amore, casomai un misto di ammirazione e di sospetto; ammirazione perché era alta, viragine e baffuta – penso fosse sui trenta – durante la guerra era stata infermiera, nel suo salotto c'eran sui muri bandierine e fotografie, una che lei era dietro la Regina tra colletti alti e greche di generali, c'era un quadretto con una lettera di D'Annunzio e cimeli, tutto pieno quel salotto, me lo faceva vedere con orgoglio quando le portavo le uova e le primizie dell'orto, "i ricordi della Patria ... La gloria ... ". Aveva un modo virile e bello di parlare, mica da maestrina, quelle frasi da libro stampato che lei diceva me le ricordavo in fila, le ripetevo a mio padre e lui rideva: "Fandonie che non servono a niente adesso, ma sì, scrivile sul quaderno, poi da grande capirai, non fare il broncio, Annin, su, va a giocare, sì, ti do il permesso, puoi prendere la bicicletta".

E questa era vera, di acciaio, lucente, esatta e veloce, molto meglio delle faccende di frasi e parole che svanivano nella corsa: strade lunghe del vallone da scoprire, prode che si svegliano in sottili fili verdi, cespi di primule, uccelli di passo, certuni bellissimi, da correre a cercarli sulla Storia Naturale, importanti, uccelli, case, facce di bambini, strade e ruote, *cose* vere e definite che cancellano parole, difficili o ambigue parole da lasciar perdere.

Ma tuttavia la mia baffuta maestra di quinta ritornava davanti a noi ogni mattina, con la sua voce sonora e cantante, la sua taglia di femmina prepotente e i neri occhi penetranti, accesi, i suoi dettati esaltati, i suoi cerimoniali patriottardi e monarchici, i suoi ordini strambi.

Una delle ragazze più grandi era la figlia di Omodeo, ridevano una mattina lei e altre due, dissero forte alludendo alla maestra: "È l'amica del signor Ferrera, ci va a letto. Con tutti quei poderi non possono soffrire i bolscevichi, guai a toccarci il signor Ferrera alla maestra". Le guardavo esterrefatta e Mariotta, la più proterva, mi apostrofò:

"Va via tu, spiona tu, che sei una signora con la bicicletta."

"Non è vero" scattai io selvaggiamente. "Mio padre è socialista come Omodeo, non è un signore mio padre."

"Un socialista col culo nella poltrona, mica lavora tuo padre. Malato! Ma va che è lustro e grasso. Mica come noi che, ogni giorno, alla bassora andiamo nei campi, altro che il dettato e il diario."

Ne aveva di lingua Mariotta, come una vecchia comare, ma più di quelle parole non arrivò a dire; dopo un attimo di perplessità mi trovai su di una seggiola vicina per prendere l'abbrivio di un balzo da gatta, fare una spaccata per aria nel balzo e abbrancarla con le gambe alla vita, giù terra a rotolarsi e menarla di pugni selvaggi sul viso. Presa così all'improvviso lei era rimasta sotto, imbrogliata nelle sottane che già portava lunghe, sotto le mie ginocchia i suoi seni molli. Quando lei riuscì a darmi una sventola nel naso sentii il fiotto del sangue che veniva e solo la gola le vidi, gliel'avevo agguantata e con l'altra mano le artigliavo capelli; lei per levarsi quella mano dalla gola armeggiava e a calci tentava rovesciarmi.

Non avevo mai fatto baruffe grosse prima, mai adoperato le mani a picchiare sodo, nemmeno le bestie (quelle, figurarsi, le amavo "come parenti"). A ben considerare, di baruffe vere non ne avevo neppure vedute e ora questo arraffare selvaggio, questi calci spietati mi venivano esatti, veloci, pesanti, lei urlava alto, acuto come se la scannassero, io ansavo senza voce, a colpi le sputavo in faccia il sangue che mi fiottava dal naso, colpivo e tiravo come presa in una rossa nuvola di pazzia e di morte.

Di quei minuti di baruffa mi resta ora come un senso acido, metallico di sangue nella bocca e le urla atroci di lei, alte sul vociare e gridare delle altre.

Ci divisero, non so chi, la bidella o la maestra, un catino d'acqua rossa per fermare il sangue dal naso a me, l'altra seduta su di una seggiola continuava un suo lagno, mentre la bidella la pettinava. La maestra di quinta, alta e minacciosa, restò in attesa fin che con un "basta" imperioso attaccò a interrogarci, martellava' domande e perché a cui non otteneva risposta, insisteva, gridava, ma più duro si faceva il nostro muro di silenzio; non conoscevamo la parola omertà, sapevamo solo per antico istinto che ora si rivelava, sapevamo la sua legge chiusa e barbara e ci facevamo maschere dure, compresse, estranee di fronte alla maestra.

"Farò venire il direttore, il parroco, il sindaco" minacciava lei "tornate accompagnate dai genitori, so io. Ma tu, Anna, dimmi, rispondi, che ti hanno fatto?"

"Storie, adesso siamo pari" mugugnai.

"Sfacciata! Oh, Dio, anche tu, ti hanno fatto diventare così sfacciata, tu con dei genitori fini e colti, tu, dimmi" mi rispose irata.

E ancora il muro del silenzio testardo, ostile, rigoroso; non concederle nemmeno un monosillabo o salterà fuori una grana, il signor Ferrera, i socialisti, i fascisti, zitto, di che si impiccia la maestra?

Infine andò a scrivere un rapporto sui quaderni, io era asserragliata in un angolo, inghiottivo sangue "per non sciuparlo", si avvicinò una ragazza con un fazzoletto pulito, lo rifiutai e adesso avevo voglia di piangere, in un singhiozzo dissi: "Tornate a dirmi spiona, provatevi" e fuggii.

Corsi giù, furiosa che mi venisse da piangere, giù nel corridoio a disincagliare la bicicletta, via, come spinta da una pazzia sgomenta, aver come tutto enorme, spaventoso come la morte, forse a Mariotta le si gonfiava il ventre per i miei calci, lei già donna, forse moriva, morivano, forse ora mi avrebbero assalita, chi non so, Mariotta, gli altri, mi sarei barricata dietro un mucchio di sassi a tirar sassi, a difendermi e uccidere. Così, come in una nebbia di orrore, ma reagendo con aggressività all'orrore, così pedalavo alla disperata verso casa attaccata al manubrio di acciaio lucente come se volessi sollevarlo, tirando dal naso moccio e sangue, inghiottendo tutto a bocconi aspri. Correre, arrivare alla conca del grembo di mia madre.

[...]
Con loro il ricordo della baruffa con Mariotta, altre cose, cose oscure, come labirinti tortuosi dove si perdeva la mente, sere lunghe, ore brutte e schifose certi giorni, con loro non c'era nulla di questo; certe volte, in certe sieste cantavano canzoni e certe marce bellissime, diceva Mario: "Noi tre, adesso, cantiamo: Berto fa il primo e tu la voce sottile; Anna, non stonare, assassina! Questa pupa deve farsi l'orecchio, impara le note, da brava, senti".

Il pezzo forte di Mario era *Addio Lugano bella* e quello di Berto *Bandiera rossa*, certe volte si mettevano a baruffare per via di faccende di anarchici e socialisti. A me soprattutto piaceva una marcia dal ritmo travolgente; venne fuori mio padre un giorno, adesso stava benino, s'era seduto sulla carriola rovesciata e l'aria di aprile gli aveva arrossato le gote come quando era più giovane e non aveva tanti mali; come omaggio Mario attaccò proprio quella canzone, mio padre si mise a seguirli, aveva la voce un po' roca, poi si sciolse, andò alto nel ritornello dell'*Internazionale.*

Restò un po' pensieroso sulla carriola e disse col suo modo un po' stanco, staccato:

"Bei tempi, quando s'era studenti, giovanotti che si credeva, nell'*Internazionale* e tante altre utopie."

"Tornano adesso quei tempi" disse forte Berto. "Tornano, vedrà, dottore, stavolta non ce la cavano via la rivoluzione."

Mio padre si strinse nelle spalle, un moto di dubbio delle sopracciglia, si alzò in silenzio e andò a vedere i lavori, si misero a parlare riguardo al vano di una finestra.

[...]

[...]

Now that I was in the fifth grade, I would go to school in the mornings, but I considered it a stupid necessity. I only did it so that I could be done with it. Of the fifteen girls, one group was small, shy, and vapid; five or six others however, were taller, with breasts already visible behind their aprons, hair put up in buns with hairpins, two or three of whom would talk amongst themselves, gossiping and cracking jokes. “Troublemakers,” my mother called them, adding sternly, “I give you the bicycle so that you can come home immediately, without ganging up [*far lega*] with them and getting into trouble along the way; I know what happens. Go and come straight back, got it?”

A bicycle was a very important thing to have; only three of us rode them and the other two lived far away, on the other side of the river.

Sometimes, my teacher would have me deliver a few letters, which I did gladly: the teacher is always the teacher.

I didn’t have any particular love for this fifth-grade teacher, however, more a mixture of admiration and suspicion: admiration because she was tall and masculine, with a moustache—I think she was in her thirties. During the war she had been a nurse, and in her living room there were little flags and photographs on the walls: one of them showed her standing behind the queen, between the high collars and insignias of generals. There was a small frame with a letter from D’Annunzio and other memorabilia; she would show me this packed living room full of pride when I brought her eggs and the first produce from our garden, recalling, “The memories of our country ... The glory ...” She had a beautiful, virile way of speaking, not at all teacherly; I would diligently memorize the sentences from the printed books she read to me; when I would repeat them to my father, he would laugh, “Oh, that rubbish has no use now, but yes, write them down in your notebook, you’ll understand when you're older. Don't sulk, Annin, go, go play, yes, you have my permission, you can take the bicycle."

And it was real! Steel, shiny, precise, and fast, much better than the affairs of words and phrases, which vanished in the wind: there were long roads to discover in the valley, pastures that unraveled like fine green threads, bouquets of primroses, migratory birds, some of utter beauty, important, worthy of being researched in the natural history books, birds, houses, faces of children, roads and wheels, real and definite *things* that erase words, difficult and ambiguous words, which are forgotten.

But still my moustached fifth-grade teacher would appear before us every morning, with her dulcet and sonorous voice, her imposing female size, her bright and piercing black eyes, her proud dictations, her patriotic and monarchical ceremonies, her peculiar orders.

One of the tall girls was Omodeo's daughter; one morning, laughing with two of the others, she said loudly, alluding to the teacher, "She's Mr. Ferrera's friend, she sleeps with him. With all those farms he owns, he can't stand the Bolsheviks; never speak ill of Mr. Ferrera in front of the teacher." I looked on in astonishment as Mariotta, the daughter of Omodeo and the most arrogant of the bunch, turned to me angrily.

"Hit the road, spy. Keep pretending to be a lady with that bicycle."

"I'm not!" I snapped back audaciously. "My father is a socialist like Omodeo, my father is not a 'gentleman.'"

"A socialist with his ass in an armchair! Your father doesn't work. Sick? He's all shiny and fat. We go to the fields each day at dawn while you sit at home with your dictations and your diaries."

Though Mariotta had a tongue like an old hag, she wasn't able to get out any more words; after a moment of perplexity, I found myself crouched on a nearby chair, preparing to pounce; as I leapt, I split open my legs, grabbing her by the waist and pulling her down to the ground, rolling and punching her wildly in the face. Having taken her by surprise, I kept her to the ground, harnessing her by her long skirt, her soft breasts beneath my knees. When she managed to slap me, I felt the blood flow; seeing her throat, I seized her there, snatching her hair in my other hand; she struggled, kicking and thrashing as she tried to throw me off her.

I had never fought before, never thrown punches with my hands, not even at the animals (on the contrary, I loved them "like a parent"). In retrospect, I had never even seen a real fight before that moment; now, in the heat of it, my blows met their mark, fast and heavy; she cried out as if she were being slaughtered; I panted wordlessly and spat the blood that was pouring out of my nose into her face; I struck and pulled at her as if caught in a red cloud of madness and death.

All that remains from that fight is an acrid taste, metallic like the blood I swilled, and her dreadful shrieks, rising above the shouts and cries of the others.

I'm not sure who separated us, either the school janitor or our teacher. Once we were apart our teacher gave me a bowl of water to stop my nosebleed while the janitor comforted Mariotta, who whined as she sat on a chair away from me. The fifth-grade teacher waited, tall and menacing, biding her time until, with an imperious, "Enough!" she began to interrogate us, hammering us with questions. When she received no answer, she dug further, but the more she screamed, the firmer our wall of silence became; we hadn't learned the term *omertà*, but we knew by ancient instinct that which now revealed itself to us, the barbaric law by which we locked ourselves together, making ourselves solid, compressed, foreign against the teacher.[1]

"I'll get the director, the parish priest, the mayor!" she threatened, "You'll come back with your parents, I'm sure. But you, Anna, tell me, what have they done to you?

"It doesn't matter, we're even now," I mumbled.

"Insolent child! Oh God, they've made you insolent, too, you with your fine, cultured parents. Tell me!" she demanded angrily.

And again the wall of silence held, stubborn, hostile, and unmovable; not one syllable would be given to her lest there be trouble. Mr. Ferrera, the socialists, the fascists—quiet!—what business was it of hers?

By the time the teacher went off to make her report in the school's record books, I was barricaded in a corner, swallowing blood "so as not to waste it." One of the girls approached me with a clean handkerchief, which I refused, feeling like I was about to cry. A sob broke out, I sputtered, "Call me a spy again, try me," and escaped.

I ran downstairs, furious that I was crying, down the corridor to untie my bicycle, off, as if driven by a frightened madness, everything around me appearing enormous, as frightening as death, perhaps Mariotta's belly was swollen from my kicks, perhaps she, already a woman, was dying, they were dying, maybe now they would attack me, I don't know who, Mariotta, the others, I would barricade myself behind a pile of stones and throw them, to defend myself and to kill. I pedaled desperately, as if overtaken by a fog of horror that I was aggressively attempting to clear, pulling on the shiny steel handlebars as if I wanted to lift them out, inhaling snot and blood from my nose, swallowing it all in bitter mouthfuls. Running, to reach the valley of my mother's lap.

[...]

The memory of the fight with Mariotta settled amongst other dark things, tortuous labyrinths along which the mind would get lost on long evenings or during the bad and rotten hours of certain days; none of this mattered to them; sometimes they would sing songs during our siestas, sometimes beautiful marches; Mario would speak, "The three of us, now, let's sing: Berto will do the tenor and you'll do the alto, Anna, don't lose the melody, you killer! This chick needs to get her ears tuned! Listen to the notes now, be a good girl."

Mario's favorite was the "Addio Lugano bella" while Berto's was the "Bandiera rossa"; sometimes they would fight over the differences between the anarchists and the socialists. I especially liked the marches with their passionate rhythms. One day, when he was doing alright, my father came outside, sitting down on the upturned wheelbarrow and letting the April breeze redden his cheeks like it had when he was younger and not in so much pain; in tribute, Mario broke into song; my father joined, following close behind. Though hoarse, his voice burst high when they reached the chorus of the "Internazionale."

Wistfully, he spoke from his seat on the wheelbarrow, sounding tired, detached.

"Ah, to be a student again, a young man believing in the 'Internazionale' and many other utopias."

"Those times are coming back," Berto said forcefully. "They're coming back, doctor, you'll see, this time the revolution isn't going to go away."

With a doubtful look on his brow, my father shrugged. Standing up in silence, he went over to inspect the men's work. Then they began to speak about the space for the window.

[...]

1 *Omertà* is a dialectal expression for the refusal to provide testimony about criminal activity, originating in the code of silence of the Mafia.

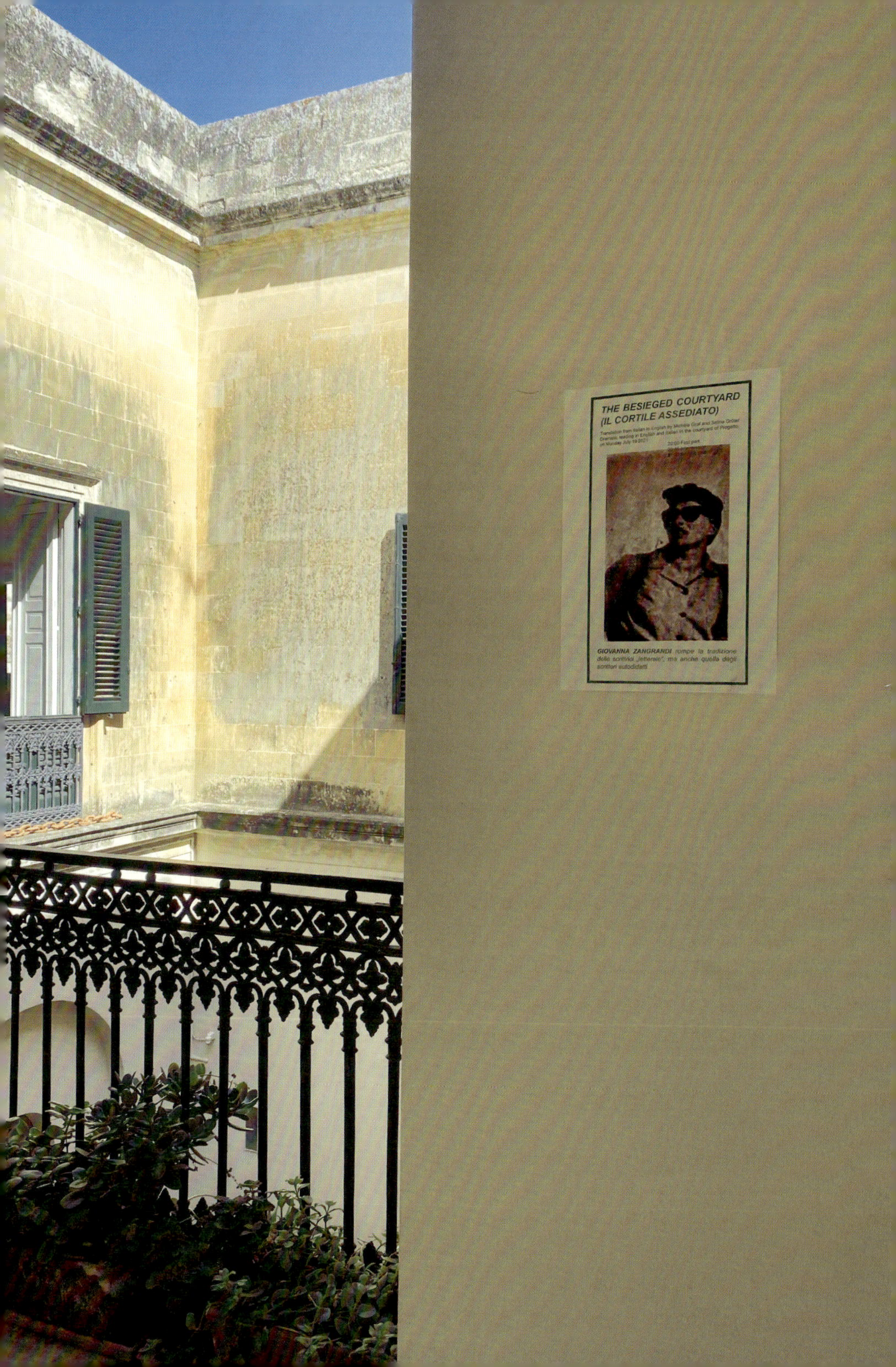

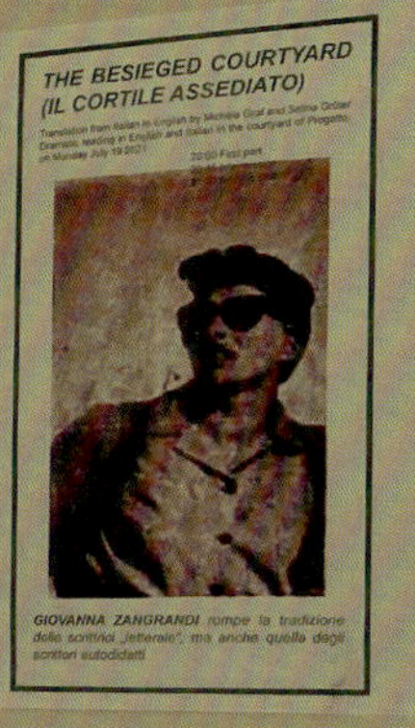
THE BESIEGED COURTYARD
(IL CORTILE ASSEDIATO)
GIOVANNA ZANGRANDI rompe la tradizione

Constellations

Noah Barker

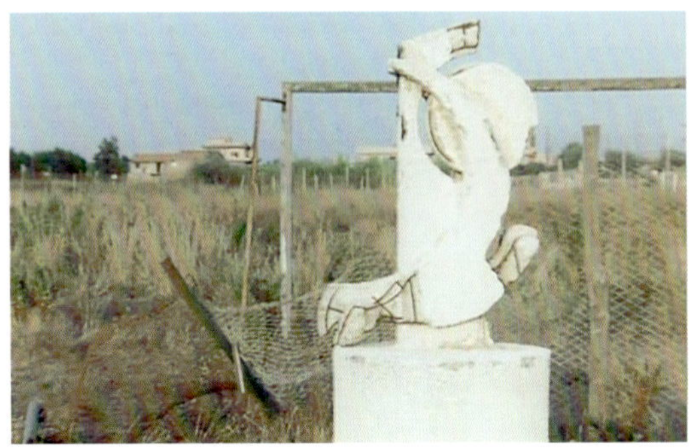

Caro Diario (Dear Diary), Nanni Moretti, 1993
Pasolini memorial at the site of his assassination

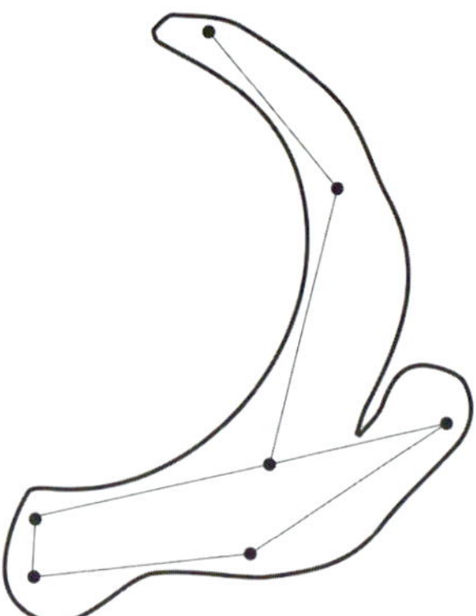

Dove
7 stars

Noah Barker

Constellation #2, 2021/2022

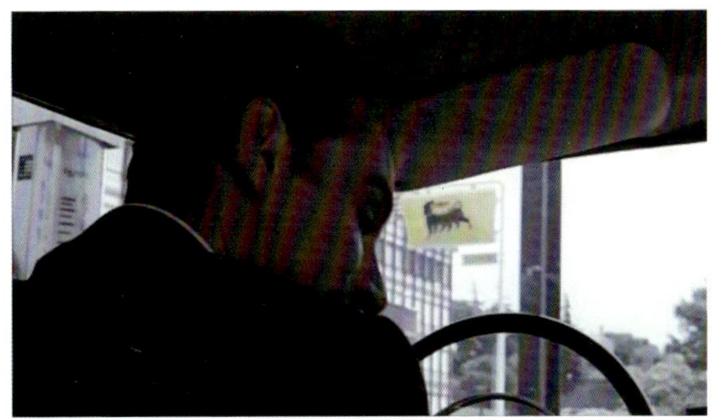

Il caso Mattei (The Mattei Affair), Francesco Rosi, 1972
Piazzale Supercortemaggiore, Metanopoli

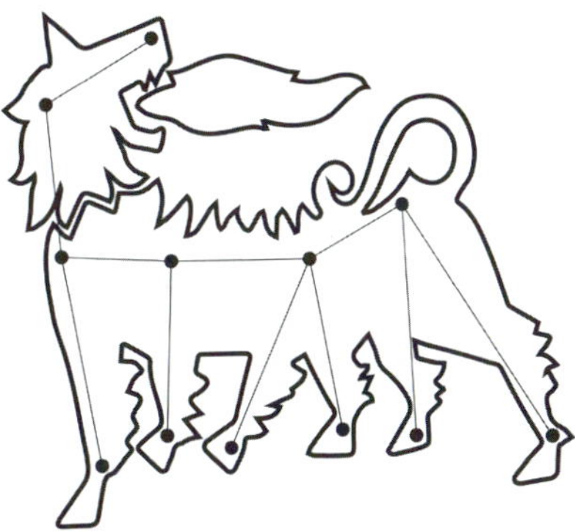

Six-legged Dog
12 stars

Noah Barker

Constellation #3, 2021/2022

A Partnership for the Future

Niloufar Emamifar

I

Cuius est solum, eius est usque ad coelum.

UNITED STATES *v.* CAUSBY ET UX.

CERTIORARI TO THE COURT OF CLAIMS.

No. 630. Argued May 1, 1946.—Decided May 27, 1946.

Respondents owned a dwelling and a chicken farm near a municipal airport. The safe path of glide to one of the runways of the airport passed directly over respondents' property at 83 feet, which was 67 feet above the house, 63 feet above the barn and 18 feet above the highest tree. It was used 4% of the time in taking off and 7% of the time in landing. The Government leased the use of the airport for a term of one month commencing June 1, 1942, with a provision for renewals until June 30, 1967, or six months after the end of the national emergency, whichever was earlier. Various military aircraft of the United States used the airport. They frequently came so close to respondents' property that they barely missed the tops of trees, the noise was startling, and the glare from their landing lights lighted the place up brightly at night. This destroyed the use of the property as a chicken farm and caused loss of sleep, nervousness and fright on the part of respondents. They sued in the Court of Claims to recover for an alleged taking of their property and for damages to their poultry business. The Court of Claims found that the Government had taken an easement over respondents' property and that the value of the property destroyed and the easement taken was $2,000; but it made no finding as to the precise nature or duration of the easement. *Held:*

1. A servitude has been imposed upon the land for which respondents are entitled to compensation under the Fifth Amendment. Pp. 260–267.

(a) The common law doctrine that ownership of land extends to the periphery of the universe has no place in the modern world. Pp. 260, 261.

(b) The air above the minimum safe altitude of flight prescribed by the Civil Aeronautics Authority is a public highway and part of the public domain, as declared by Congress in the Air Commerce Act of 1926, as amended by the Civil Aeronautics Act of 1938. Pp. 260, 261, 266.

(c) Flights below that altitude are not within the navigable air space which Congress placed within the public domain, even though they are within the path of glide approved by the Civil Aeronautics Authority. Pp. 263, 264.

$3.95

A NORTON CRITICAL EDITION

Red and Black

STENDHAL

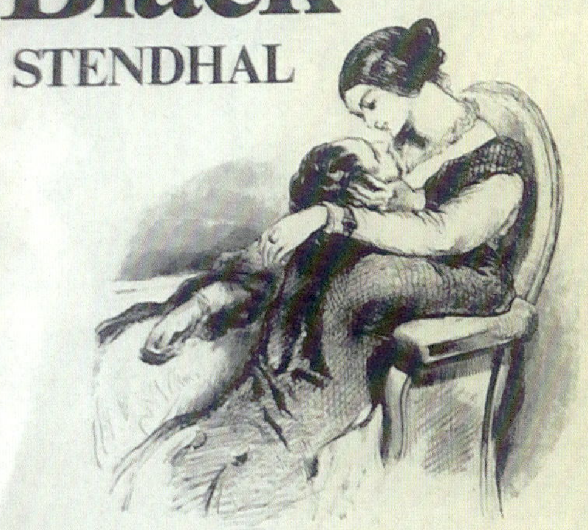

TRANSLATED AND EDITED BY
ROBERT M. ADAMS

A NEW TRANSLATION
BACKGROUNDS AND SOURCES
CRITICISM

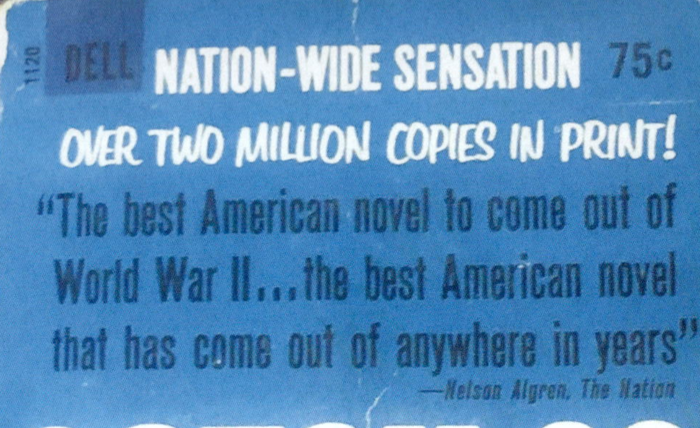

CATCH-22

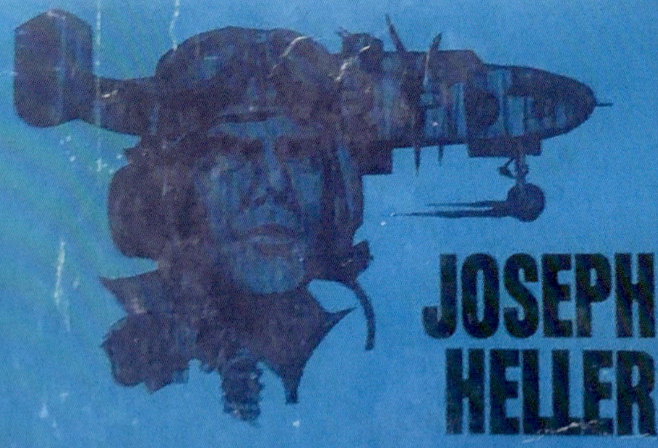

"A wild, moving, shocking, hilarious, raging, exhilarating, giant roller-coaster of a book"
—New York Herald Tribune

Ballantine/Fiction/31221/$4.95

#1
BESTSELLER

LINCOLN

A NOVEL

GORE VIDAL

"Superb... a grand entertainment... an astonishing achievement...Vidal is a masterly American historical novelist."
The New York Review of Books

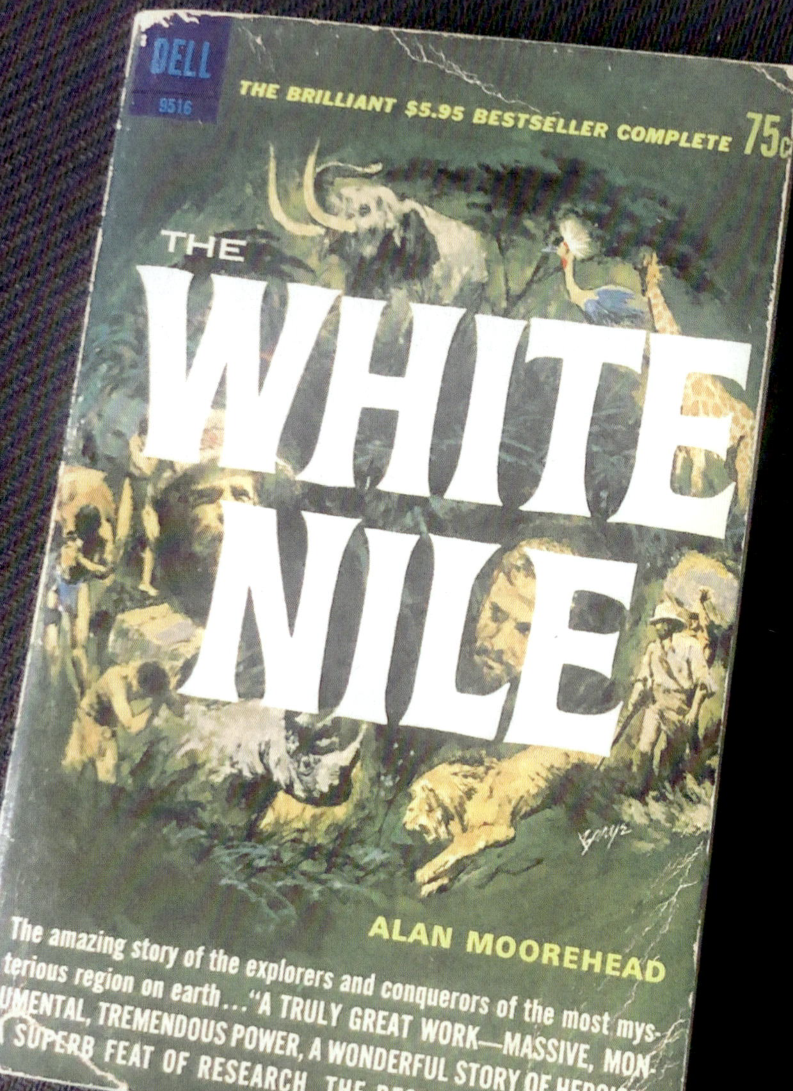
DELL
9516
THE BRILLIANT $5.95 BESTSELLER COMPLETE
75c
THE
WHITE
NILE
ALAN MOOREHEAD
The amazing story of the explorers and conquerors of the most mysterious region on earth..."A TRULY GREAT WORK—MASSIVE, MONUMENTAL, TREMENDOUS POWER, A WONDERFUL STORY OF HEROISM, A SUPERB FEAT OF RESEARCH, THE BEST BOOK OF ITS KIND"

U.S. Go Home

Stefano Faoro

Weapons, heterosexuality, the US economy, Christmas, the American Civil War, political economy, social mobility, World War II, Abraham Lincoln, colonialism, the Cold War, boyhood, comradeship, sex, the American Civil War, foreign policy, the subconscious desire to be taken care of by others, finance, the Iraq War from 2006 to 2008, sexual adjustment in marriage.

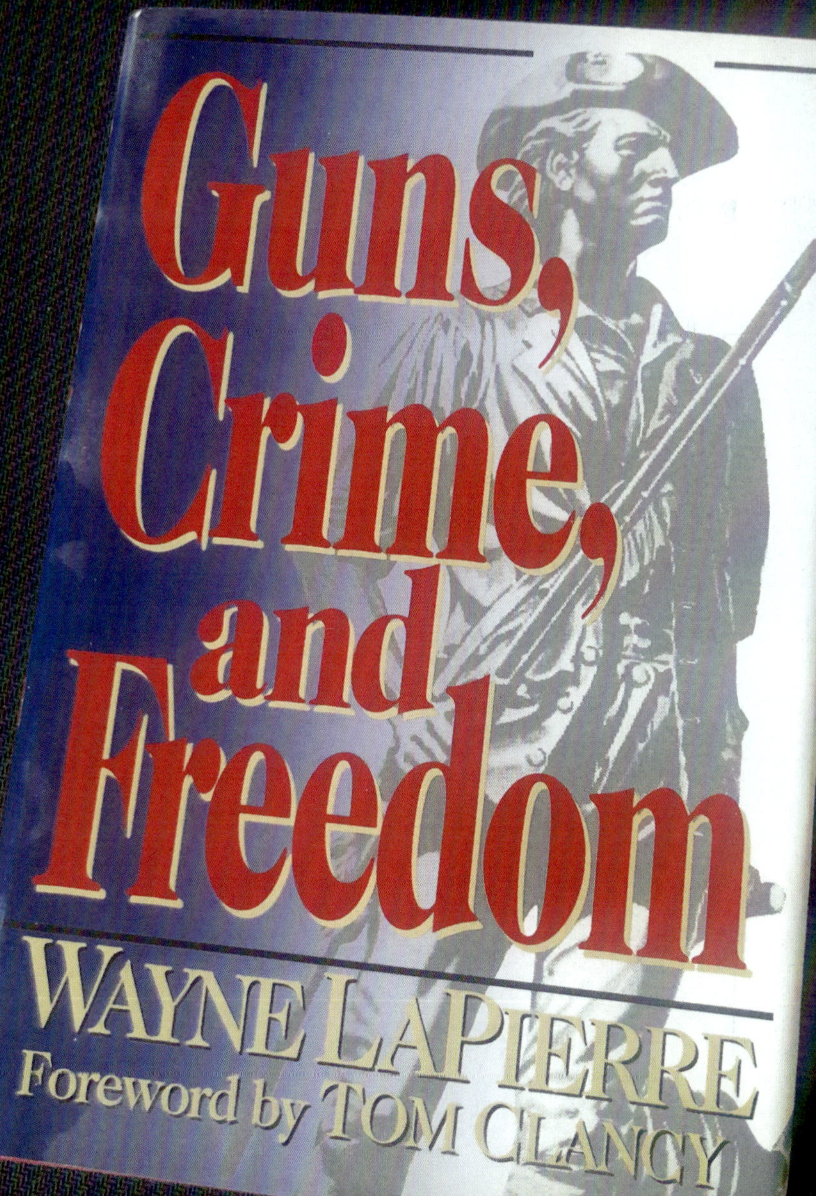
Guns,
Crime,
and
Freedom
WAYNE LAPIERRE
Foreword by TOM CLANCY

MEN ARE FROM MARS, Women Are from Venus

A Practical Guide for Improving Communication and Getting What You Want in Your Relationships

JOHN GRAY, Ph.D.

COMEBACK AMERICA

Turning the Country Around and Restoring Fiscal Responsibility

DAVID M. WALKER

President and CEO of the Peter G. Peterson Foundation and former comptroller general of the United States

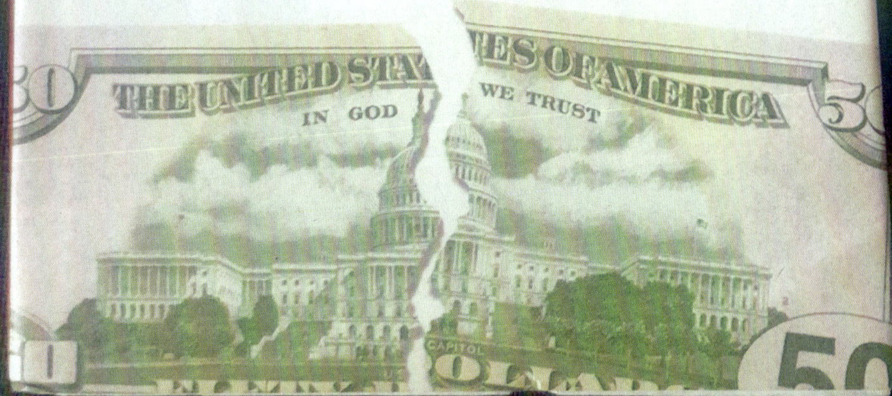

Christmas in America

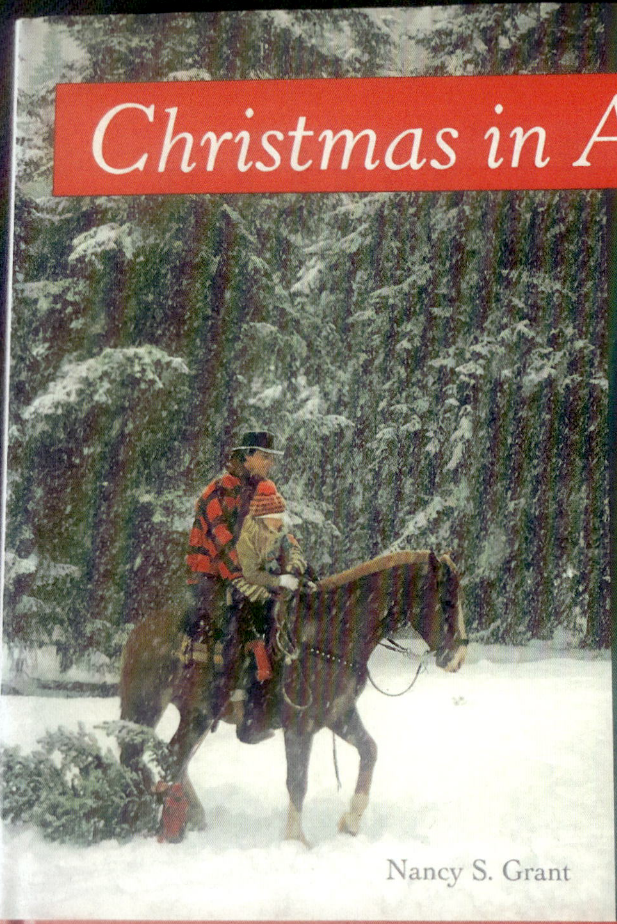

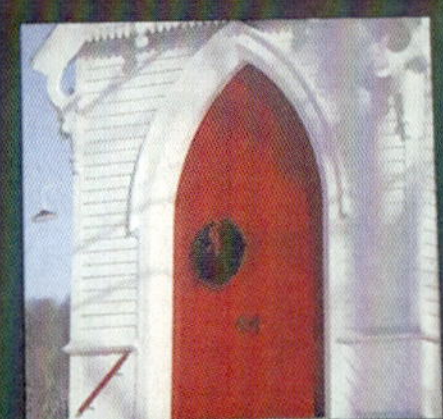

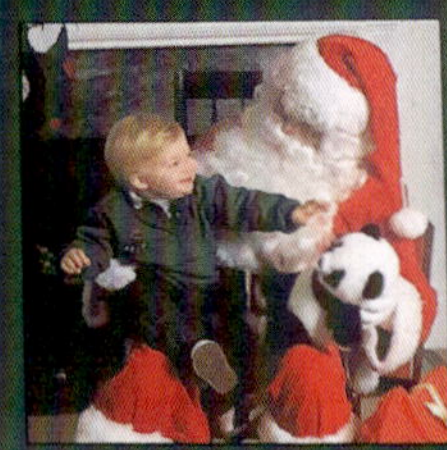

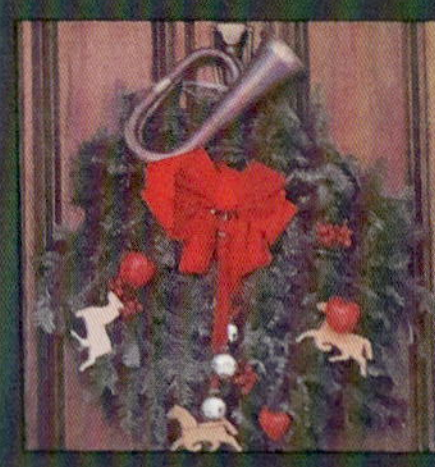

Nancy S. Grant

CHANCELLORSVILLE

Lee's Greatest Battle

EDWARD J. STACKPOLE

CAPITALISM & FREEDOM

A leading economist's view of the proper role of competitive capitalism

MILTON FRIEDMAN

P111 $1.50

The AMERICAN HERITAGE

Picture History of

THE CIVIL WAR

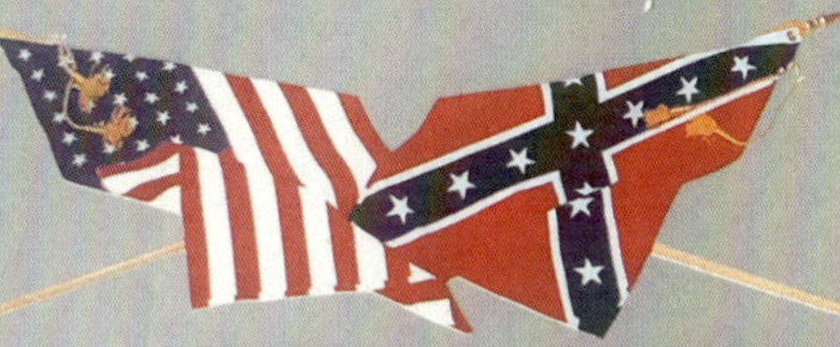

The Epic Struggle of the Blue and the Gray by the Pulitzer Prize-Winning Historian

BRUCE CATTON

DELL 1031

$1.25

NEW BLOCKBUSTING NOVEL BY THE AUTHOR OF ADVISE AND CONSENT

ALLEN DRURY

CAPABLE OF HONOR

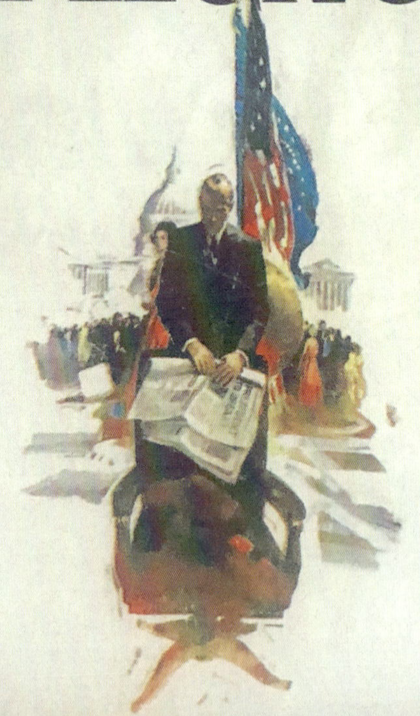

NONFICTION

OVER 1 MILLION COPIES IN PRINT!

THE CINDERELLA COMPLEX

WOMAN'S HIDDEN FEAR OF INDEPENDENCE

COLETTE DOWLING

POCKET 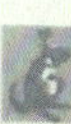 64075-5 $4.95

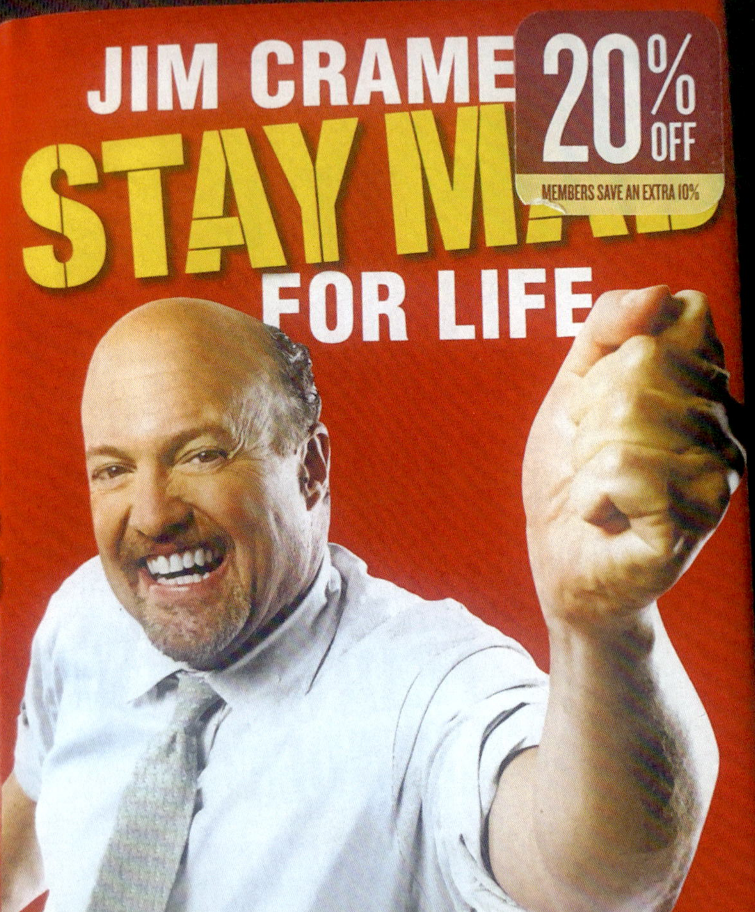

GET RICH, STAY RICH
(MAKE YOUR KIDS EVEN RICHER)

JAMES J. CRAMER WITH **CLIFF MASON**

#1 *New York Times* Bestselling Author of *Fiasco*

THOMAS E. RICKS

WINNER OF THE PULITZER PRIZE

THE GAMBLE

GENERAL DAVID PETRAEUS AND THE AMERICAN MILITARY ADVENTURE IN IRAQ, 2006–2008

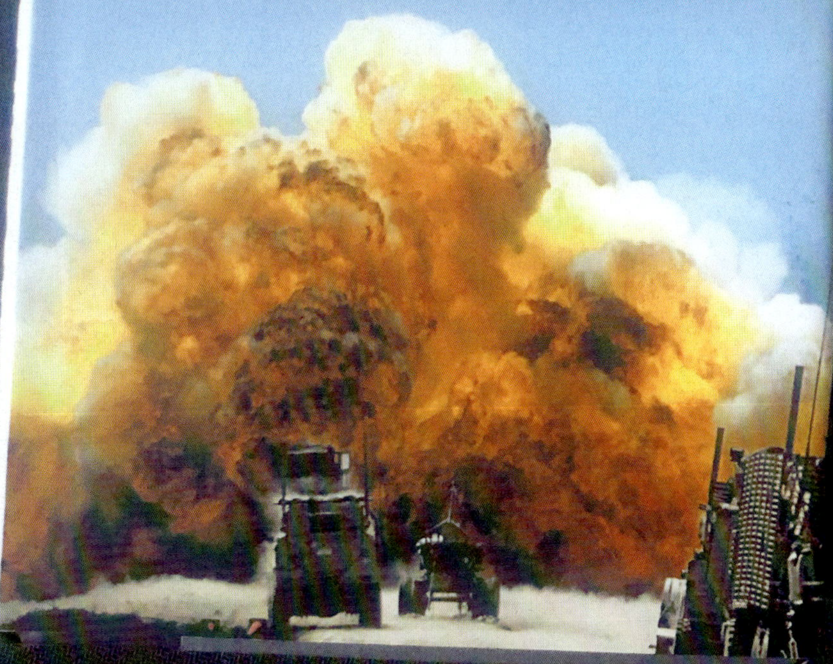

A COMPLETE GUIDE FOR SEXUAL ADJUSTMENT IN MARRIAGE

HANDBOOK FOR HUSBANDS
(AND WIVES)

NEW REVISED EDITION

PORTER DAVIS

A SOVIET SUPER SUB RACES FOR FREEDOM...
THE RUNAWAY NEW YORK TIMES BESTSELLER BY

TOM CLANCY

THE HUNT FOR RED OCTOBER

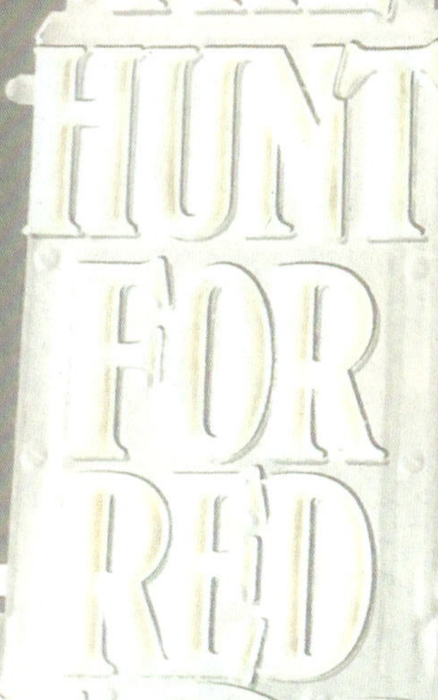

THE SUPERTHRILLER OF THE YEAR
"I COULDN'T PUT IT DOWN."—Jack Higgins

A BERKLEY BOOK · 0-425-08383-7 · ($5.95 CANADA) · $4.50 U.S.

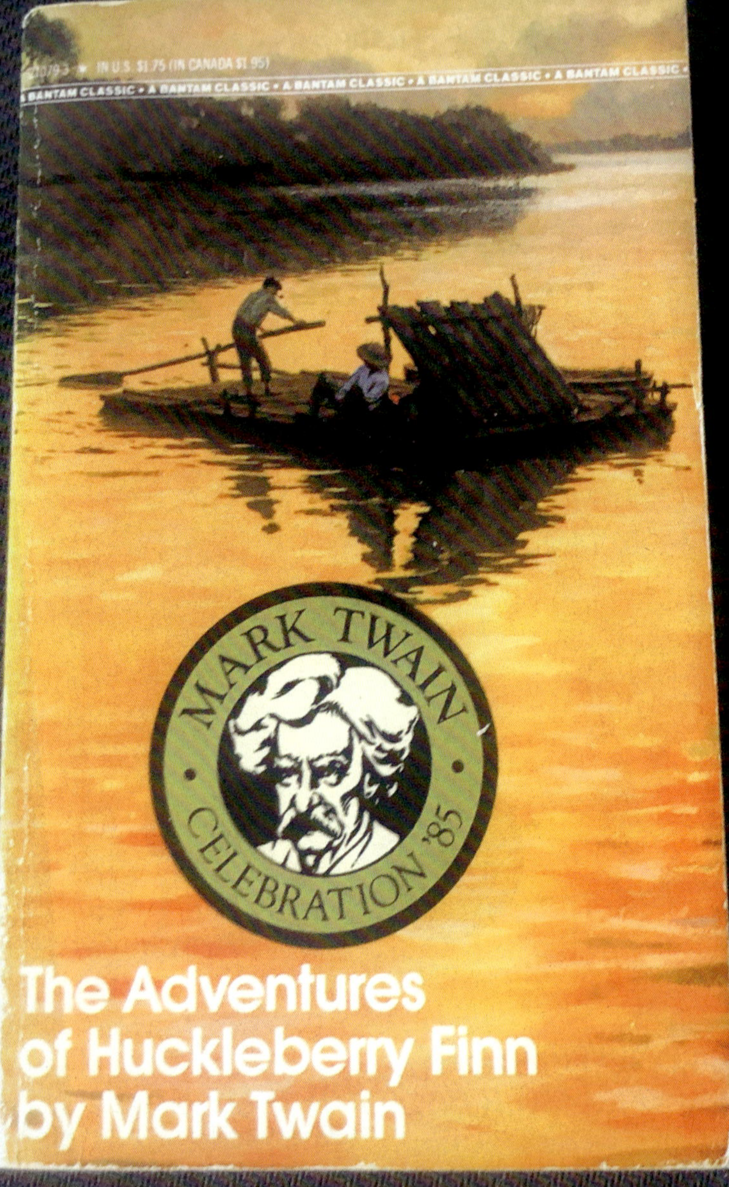

IN U.S. $1.75 (IN CANADA $1.95)
A BANTAM CLASSIC • A BANTAM CLASSIC • A BANTAM CLASSIC • A BANTAM CLASSIC • A BANTAM CLASSIC
MARK TWAIN
CELEBRATION '85
The Adventures
of Huckleberry Finn
by Mark Twain

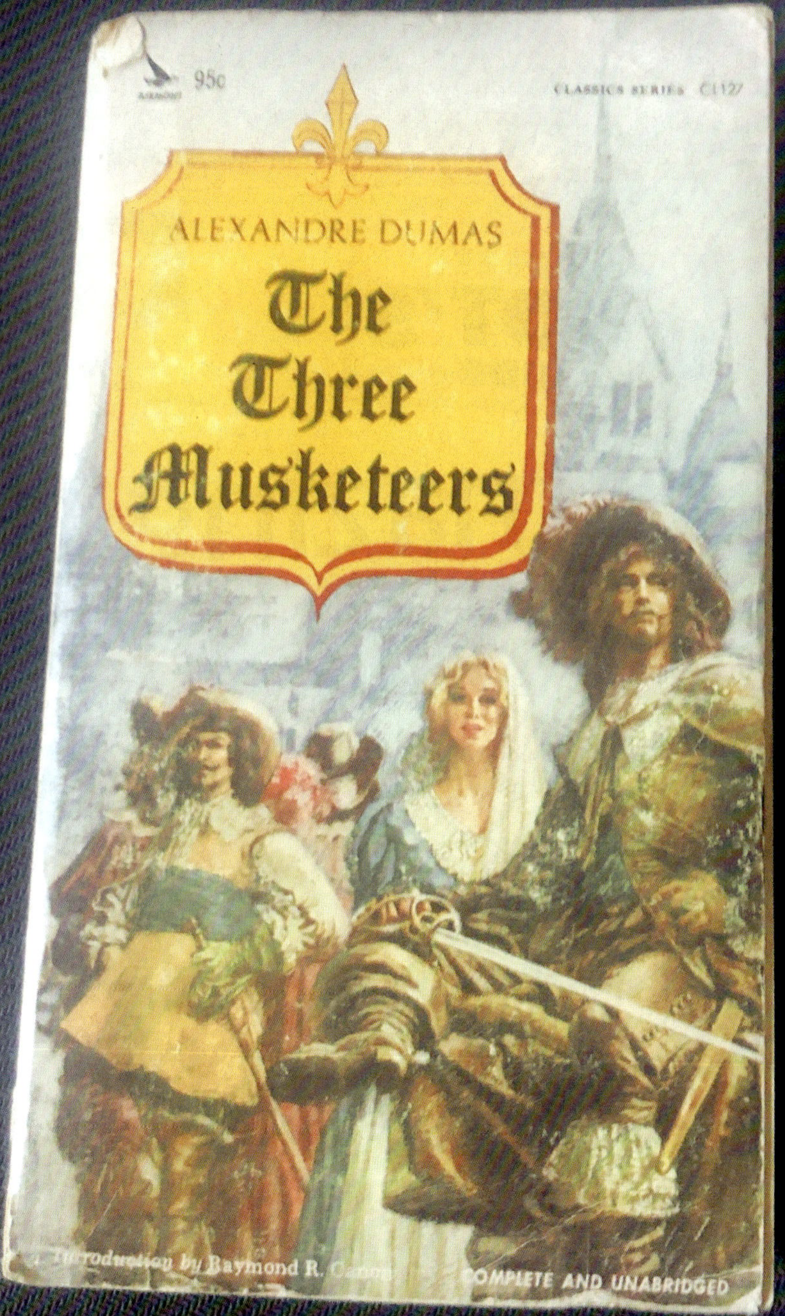

95¢

CLASSICS SERIES C1127

ALEXANDRE DUMAS

The Three Musketeers

Introduction by Raymond R. Canon

COMPLETE AND UNABRIDGED

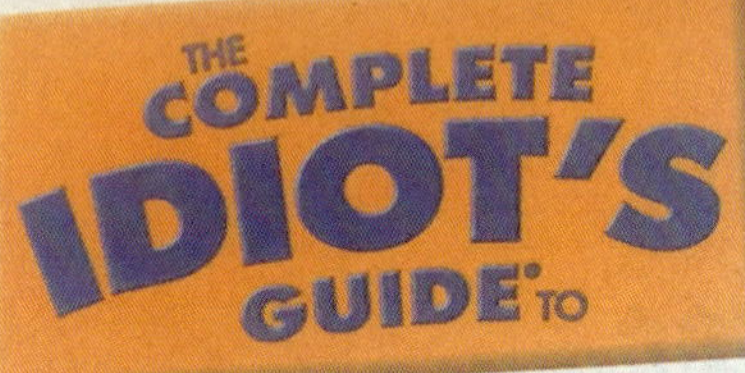

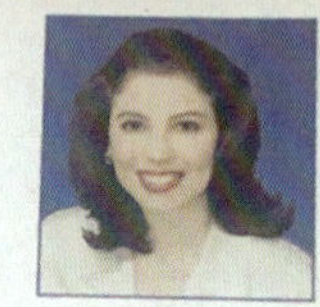

Sari Locker

Playboy magazine calls Sari Locker "our favorite tantalizing sex writer."

Amazing Sex

SECOND EDITION

- **Sensual advice** on achieving a more satisfying and exciting sex life
- **Expert explanations** to help you get past your inhibitions and express sexual creativity
- **Exotic descriptions** of sexual techniques to help you maximize your pleasure

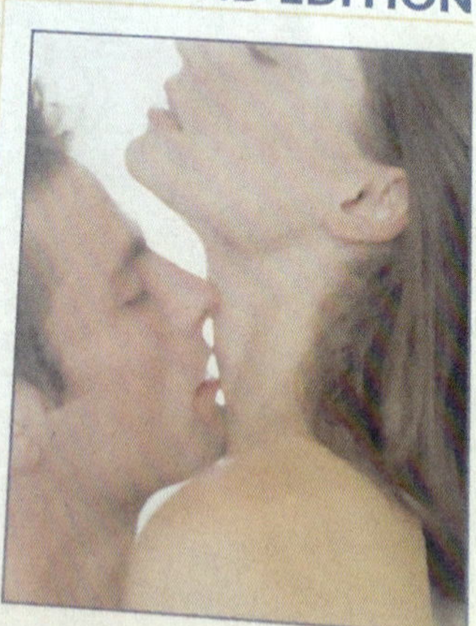

Sari Locker

Transferred unused development rights
Unused development rights on zoning lot with landmarked building
STREET

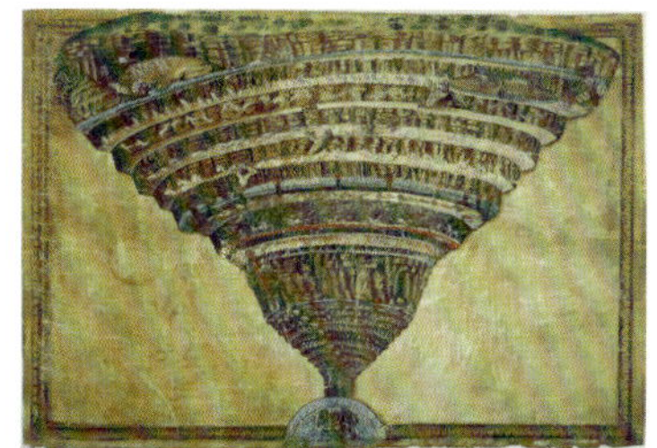

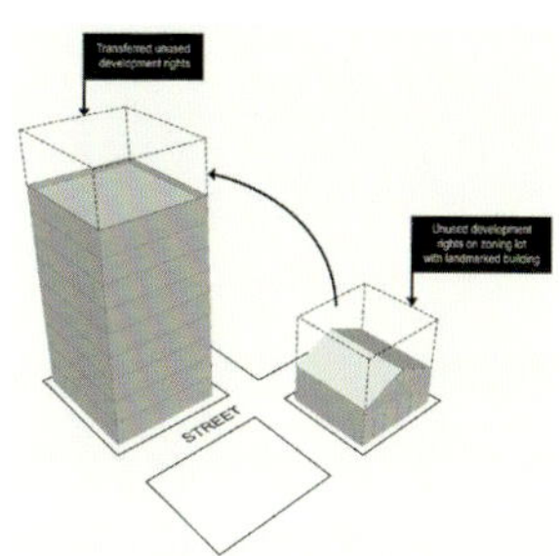

5

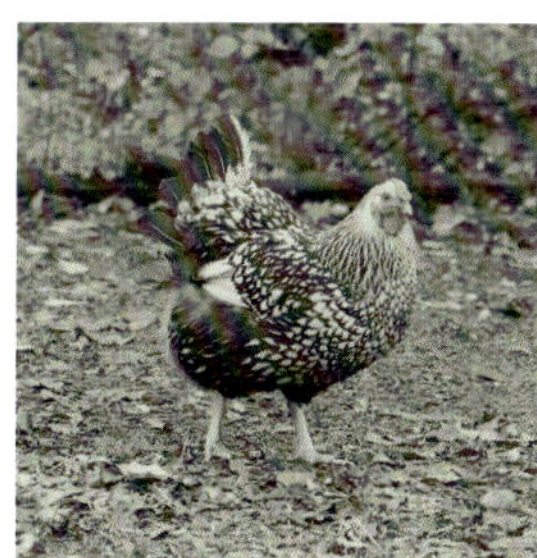

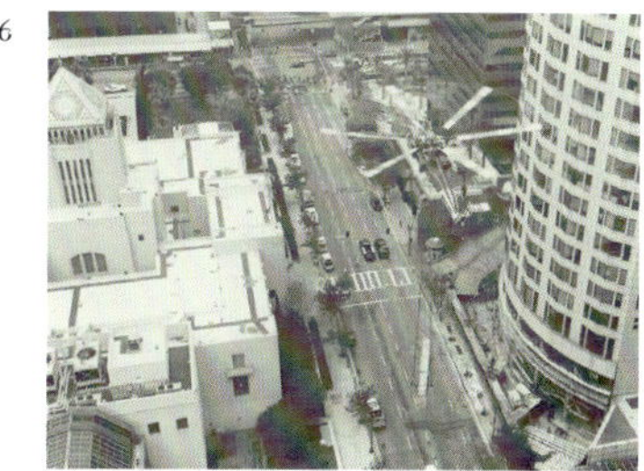

7

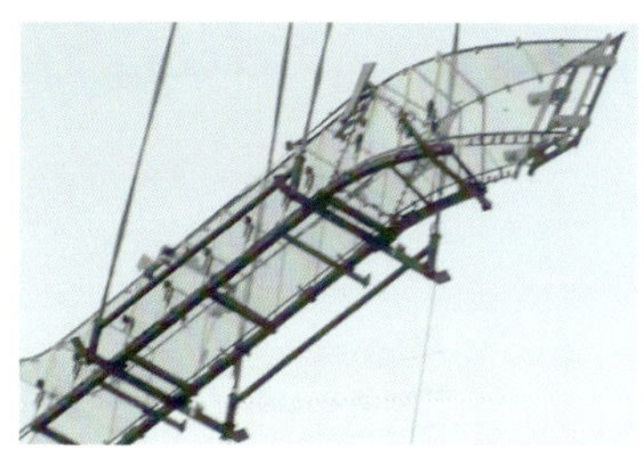

8

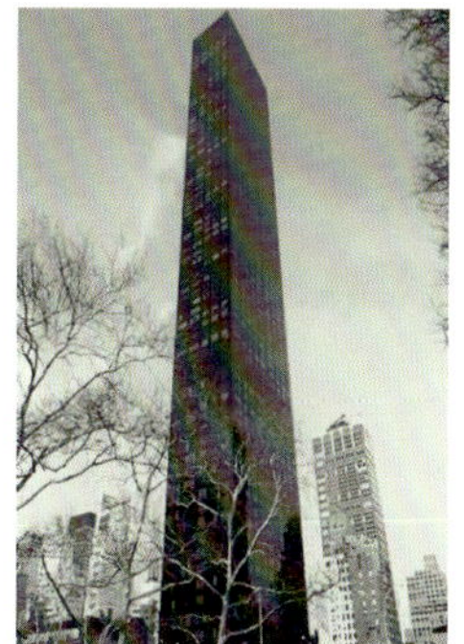

9

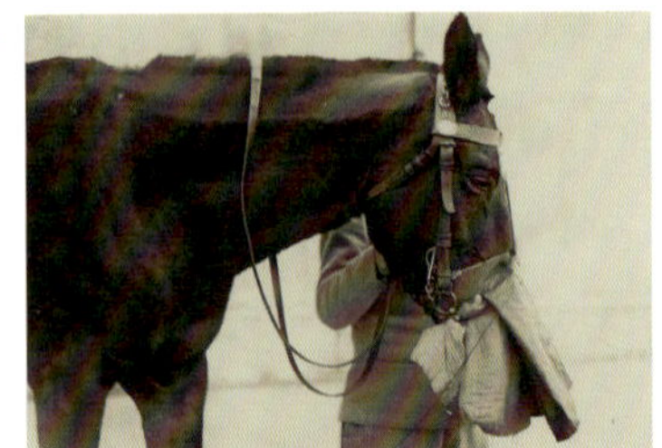

10

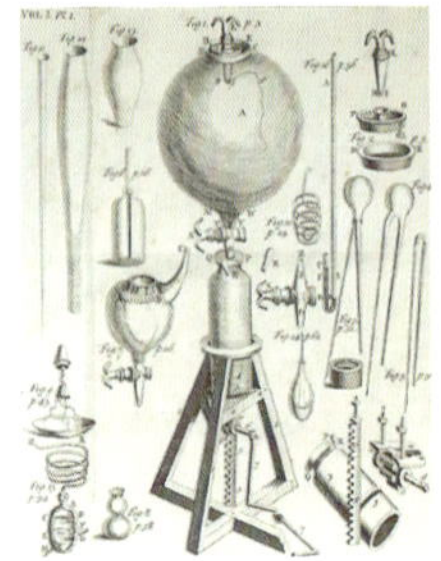

11

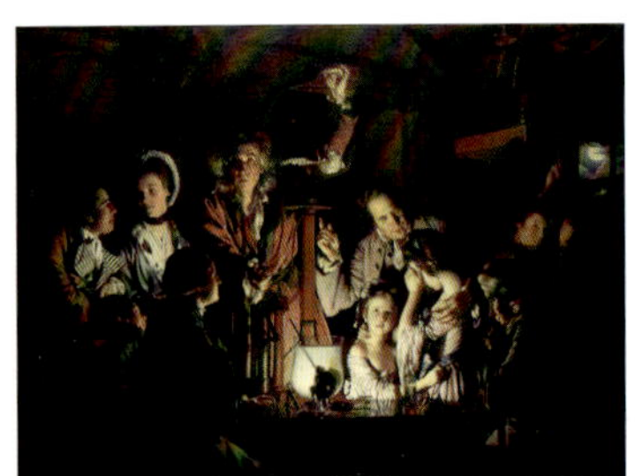

12

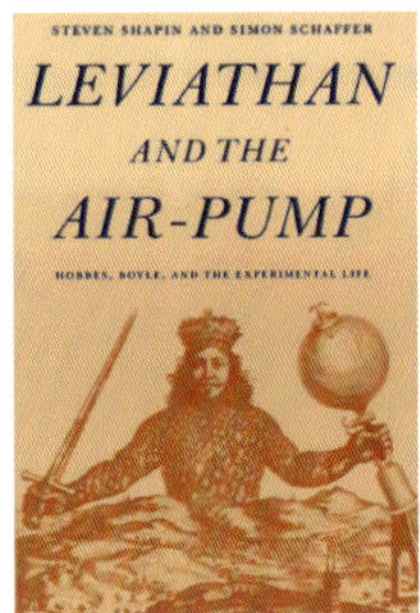

13

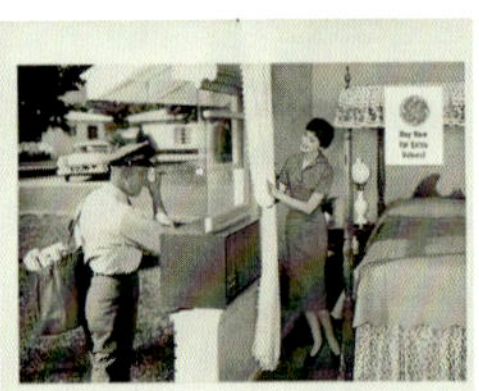

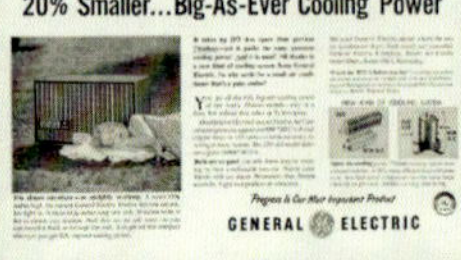

14

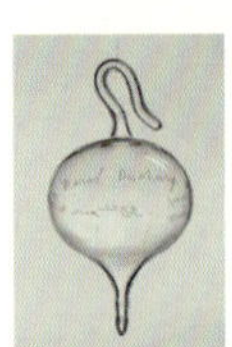

15

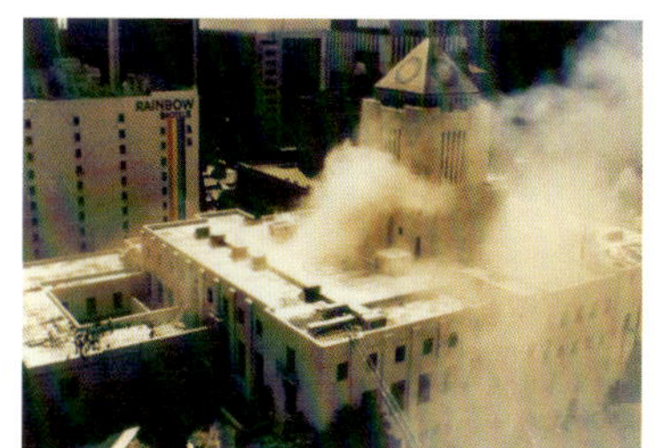

16

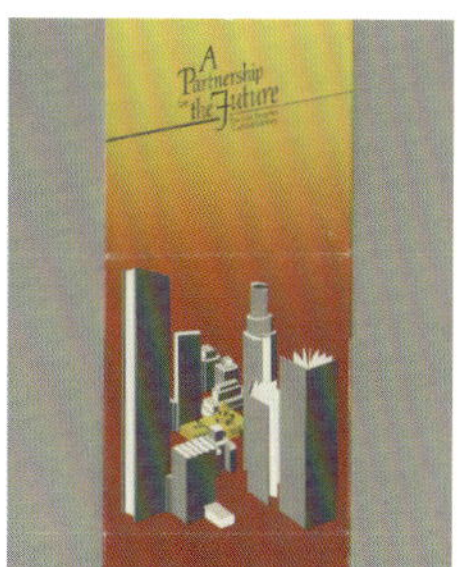

17

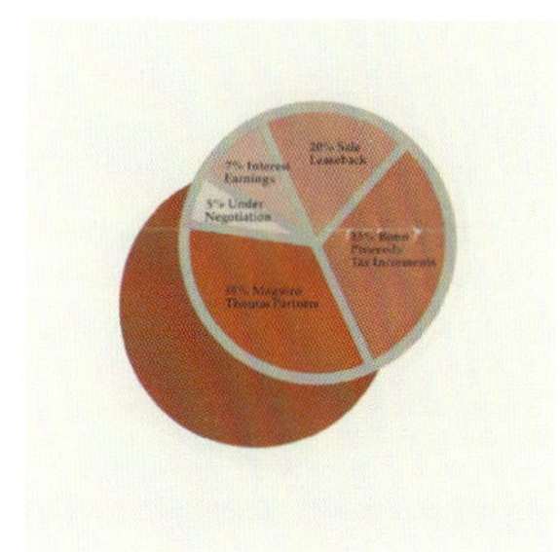

18

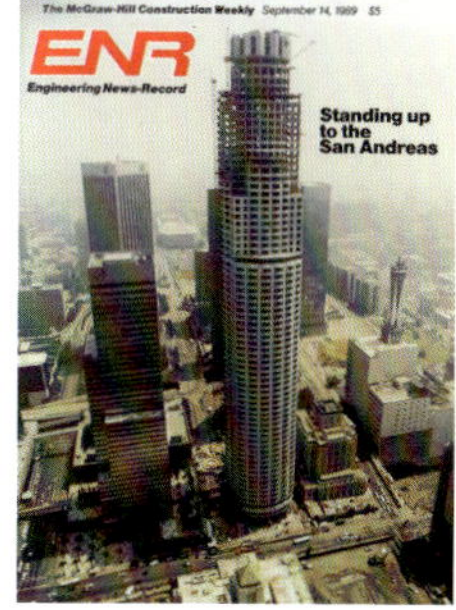

19

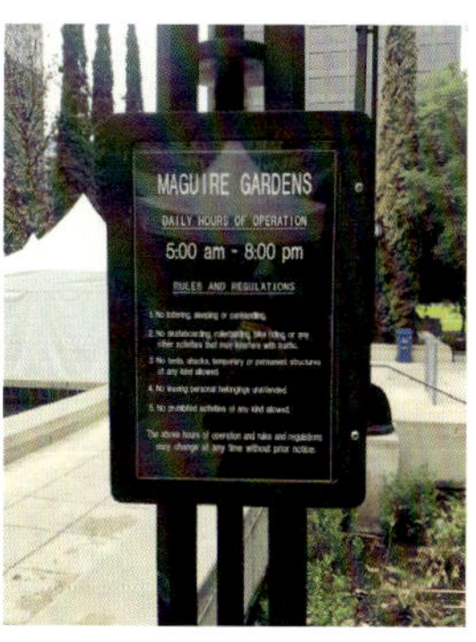

20

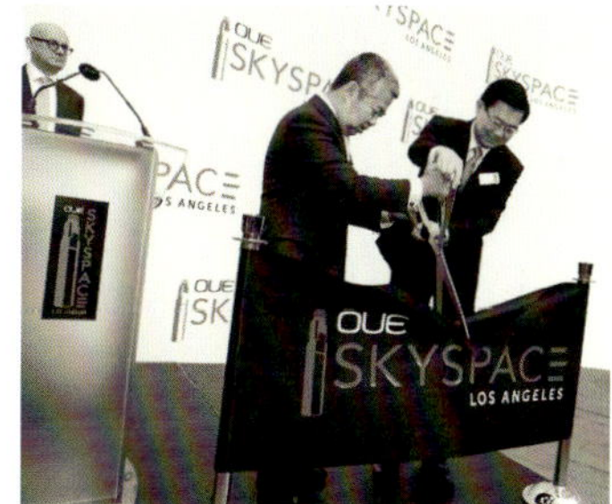

21

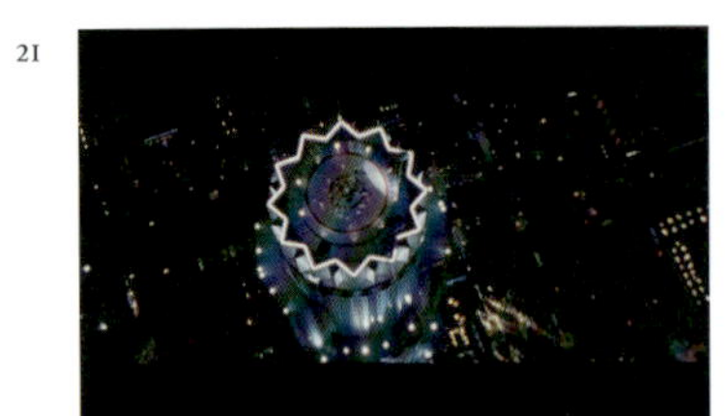

22

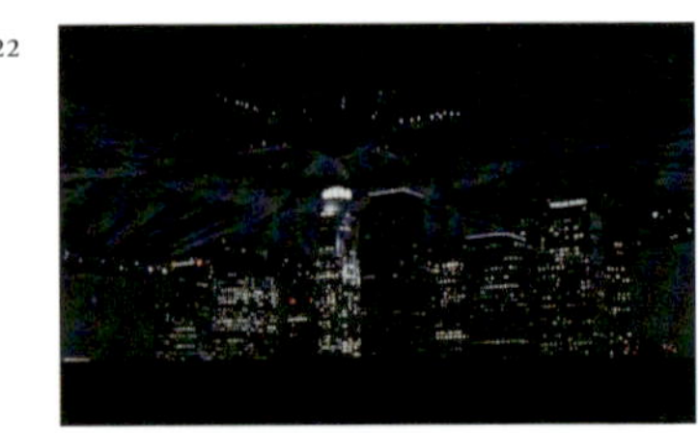

23

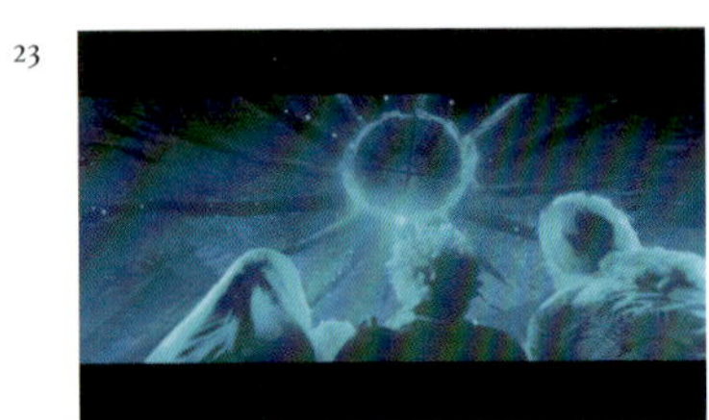

24

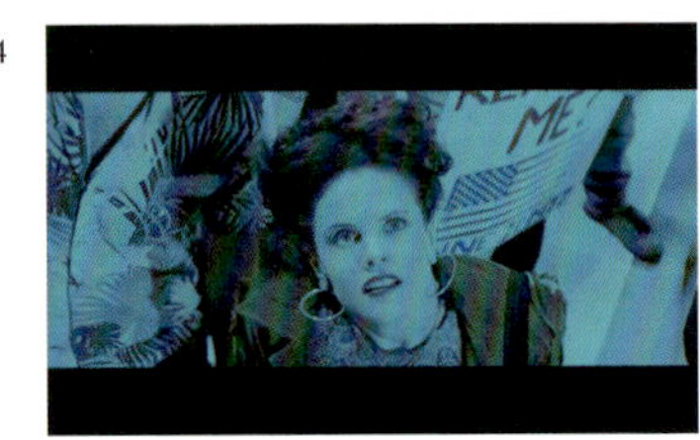

25

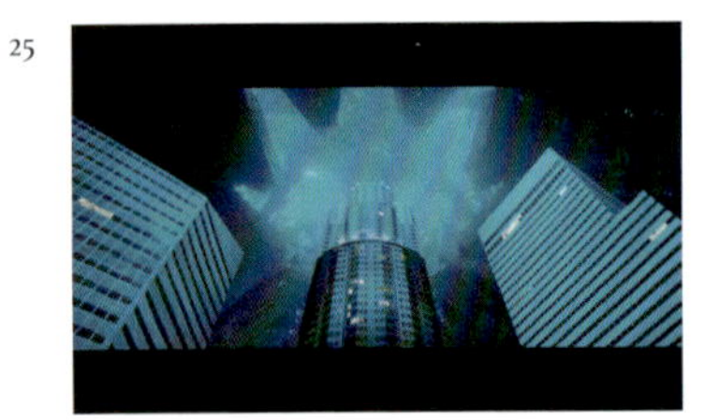

26

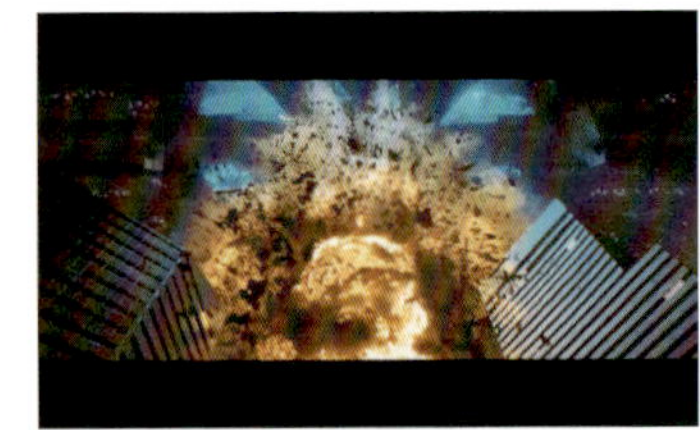

Excerpts from a lecture on the economy of view and the financial liquidity of empty space. The lecture was delivered under the open sky of Progetto via Zoom.

1 "Whoever owns the soil, it is theirs up to Heaven, and all the way down to Hell." Byron K. Elliot, "Law of the Air," *Indiana Law Journal* 6, no. 3 (December 1930): 168.

2 United States v. Causby, 328 U.S. 256 (1946).

3 Sandro Botticelli, *La mappa dell'Inferno* (The Map of Hell), 1476–1500. Silverpoint and ink on parchment. Biblioteca Apostolica Vaticana, Vatican City. In *Divina Commedia illustrata da Sandro Botticelli* by Dante Alighieri, 101r, Florence: Lorenzo di Pierfrancesco de' Medici, 1476–1500.

4 Illustration from Department of City Planning, City of New York, *A Survey of Transferable Development Rights Mechanisms in New York City*, February 26, 2015.

5 Sareh Imani, *Pooneh*, 2022.

6–7 Delivery of the Sky Slide to the Sixty-Ninth-Floor Terrace of the US Bank Tower, Los Angeles, in preparation for installation, 2016. Stills from Keath Flohr, "Sky Slide—US Bank Tower, Los Angeles, CA" (2016), YouTube, uploaded by keath flohr, March 22, 2016. Available at https://www.youtube.com/watch?v=wlEDMp76z68.

8 Donald Trump's 845 United Nations Plaza, New York, 2001. Courtesy Ysrael A. Seinuk, P.C. (YAS). Trump bought the air rights from various surrounding properties in order to build the tower, which rises 863 feet into the Manhattan skyline, in a strategy referred to as "snowballing."

9 Horse wearing a gas mask, 1914/1918. Photo by Private First Class Camille B. Fuller, 1st Corps, 1st Photo Section, AEF. National WWI Museum and Memorial, Kansas City, Missouri.

10 Boyle's air pump as depicted in *The Works of the Honourable Robert Boyle*. London: Printed for A. Millar, 1744. Foyle Special Collections, Rare Books Coll., Kings College London.

11 Joseph Wright, *An Experiment on a Bird in the Air Pump*, 1768. Oil on canvas, 183 x 244 cm. National Gallery, London. A cockatiel flutters in panic as the air is slowly withdrawn from the vessel by the pump. Photograph provided by The National Gallery/Art Resource, NY.

12 Cover of Steven Shapin and Simon Schaffer, *Leviathan and the Air-Pump: Hobbes, Boyle, and the Experimental Life*. Princeton, NJ: Princeton University Press, 1985. The book examines "the sociological study of scientific knowledge" in the works of Thomas Hobbes and Robert Boyle.

13 General Electric Air Conditioner, 1958.

14 Screenshot of Lot 14 from Christies' Live Auction 12151, May 7, 2016. An edition of Marcel Duchamp's *Air de Paris* (1919; ed. 1964) sold at the auction for $845,000. Available at https://www.christies.com/en/lot/lot-5994795.

15 Aerial view of Los Angeles Central Library fire, April 29, 1986. Security Pacific National Bank Collection, Los Angeles Public Library.

16–17 Cover and image from Los Angeles Public Library, *A Partnership for the Future*, 1986. The brochure was produced to announce the reopening of the library after the 1986 fire. For years, Maguire/Thomas Partners tried to get permission to build a seventy-three-story office building on Fifth Street across from the library. As Los Angeles had a height limitation of forty stories, however, the city refused the request. In the early 1980s, Maguire/Thomas offered to buy the library's air rights. This purchase, in addition to the forty stories Maguire/Thomas was already allowed to construct, enabled the partners to build the seventy-three-story US Bank Tower.

18 Cover of *ENR (Engineering News-Record): The McGraw-Hill Construction Weekly*, September 14, 1989. Reprinted courtesy Engineering News-Record, copyright BNP Media, all rights reserved.

19 Maguire Gardens, Los Angeles. Photo by the author.

20 Overseas Union Enterprise Limited (OUE), a Singapore-based hotel and property company run by Indonesian billionaire Stephen Riady, acquired the US Bank Tower and other related assets in Los Angeles for $367.5 million in 2013. OUE opened the tower to the public for the first time in 2016 with a reveal of the Sky Slide. In 2019, the building celebrated one million visitors, which meant that the Sky Slide had made more than $70 million in less than three years. Available at https://www.prnewswire.co.uk/news-releases/oue-unveils-oue-skyspace-la-and-first-of-its-kind-skyslide-at-us-bank-tower-300290221.html.

21–26 Stills from Roland Emmerich, *Independence Day*, 1996. Color, sound, 2h 25m. 20th Century Studios.

Why Must You Reduce Everything to Money?

Marina Vishmidt

All struggles struggle in the first place with ideology, the sense that there is a "natural" objection to whatever they are trying to do. Don't rock the boat; things are hard enough. It's an objection that is at once hostile and intimate for the people trying to decide if it is worthwhile to struggle, and to make any plans beyond continuing to obey orders. What should be emphasized, however, especially in the context of an art exhibition, and particularly in one as spatially and temporally iterative as *Autoreduction*, is the extent to which another version of how things could be, or what often gets referred to these days as "world building," is central to the practical criticism of how they are.

A hint in this direction was provided by Fredric Jameson, who wrote of Ursula K. Le Guin's *The Left Hand of Darkness* as a utopia created via reduction. In the book, Le Guin takes a limited set of variables to sketch out a panoply of suggestive political fictions in her narrative, from frigid temperatures (and the subsequent nature of sociality in a cold climate) to reduced periods of sexual availability.[1] Jameson's thought is echoed in a more metapolitical key by Jacques Rancière, who writes of the significance of "inactuality" to resistance: "One needed this radical inactuality in order to meet the inactuality which is at the core of the refusal of the 'natural' order of things, i.e. the natural order of domination."[2] There is thus not a standoff between ideology and material interests; rather, ideology runs right through what gets defined as material interests—that is to say, as "natural"—and what is then considered natural about domination.

The title *Autoreduction* is one with multiple active dimensions. The show's demystification of a solo exhibition through collaboration and a drawn-out temporality is a reduction of the "author." The term also refers to *autoriduzione*, the tactic of "price setting by riot" (among other means) in the history of Italian social-reproduction struggles. It also points to the territory of Lecce, once dominated by a heavily feminized and militant tobacco workforce, now by an agritourism complex that includes enterprises such as boutique hotels and art spaces. This carousel of capital's value-forms is slowed down in the exhibition, halted in freeze-frames: tobacco-rolling stations suspended, in Dora Budor's installation, between decay and their eventual repurposing as banquet tables; the proliferation of unprocessed debris in the Italian countryside, parsed and poised on the gallery roof by Ser Serpas (*Isn't Anything*, 2021). Such an itinerary of work, leisure, and waste is shot through with many species of ideology—"many species" because specification is important. For ideology to be a helpful analytic tool, it must be acknowledged that it is not one thing. One approach we might want to take is to see ideology as a "perceptual economy" of capital—the way things cannot help but appear in light of the social relations that prevail.[3] This is distinct from thinking of ideology as a mistake or a deception, or even as the structurally rooted gap of the "imaginary relationship of individuals to their real conditions of existence." Critique, on the other hand, bears the infamy of reduction, of bringing out one feature to narrate something definitive about a situation and thus a potential "reduction" of complexity in order to propose that something needs to change. "Why must you reduce everything to money?" is the anguished cry of the boss to whom nothing is more important than money, except perhaps for their workers' compliance. It doesn't always even come from "the boss," but it always expresses the dismissal of all struggles around the things that decide if and how we live or die. Struggles around wages, struggles around prices ... The ideological answer to all demands for more is a cry against reduction, which is always insidious. Every union-avoidant corporation that wishes its staff would voice their concerns directly to management instead of organizing is wielding a "one big happy family" ideology against the "reduction" to a capital:labor relation.

Further, divisions emerge between those who are more and less expected to be the agents of struggle. The *tabacchine* of Lecce didn't just have the bosses to reckon with. The action taken by women workers, as the Italian Autonomist feminists put it, was a "struggle within the struggle." Every time someone advances a recognition that gender or race cuts across the normative image of the worker in a patriarchal society, it risks separating workers and their struggles from one another if not directly addressed, and ultimately it can reunite them with the boss. Coming up with a plan, however, is the other side of autoreduction; that is, the *auto-* side. The autonomy to decide which prices are worth paying if at all can be collectively set by those with few resources—or resources they have decided to control. Autonomy is in this sense is not secession nor nationalism but the rationality of the oppressed, the only kind capable of spreading equality beyond its mere forms. And beyond autoreduction is the "human strike" about which Claire Fontaine have been writing, which considers what a mode of refusal as extensive as the mobilization of life that capital and state power depend upon could be like.[4]

Autoreduction as a withdrawal of the power of price setting from the market is a way of profaning the market's deified status. It is at the same time an evacuation of the sacred entity of the customer, and it performs a similar reducing of oneself to the function of exchange that industrial action does, only this time in the marketplace. This zero point of interaction between the person (as a worker and/or consumer) and capital is the starting point of expansion into collective struggle. The reduction enacted by this refusal, with its correlate of autonomization, or the building of independent power, as against the autonomy of money that otherwise prevails, should be compared to the "self-optimization" of human capital that is in fact only a running in place or digging a hole deeper. Autoreduction should thus be juxtaposed to speculation—self-fashioning as capital value—as a form of self-expansion or self-development in line with the ideology of the win-win, the common sense of exploitation that unites capital and labor. The image that would correspond is the frictionless conversion of industrial heritage into luxury tourism, where artistic labor is strictly part of the upgrade.

Thus we see that there is a dialectic between the struggle against domination as a bid to expand possible worlds and change the relations of the world, and the struggle against the ideology that disparages such efforts as "reductive." To expand is to reduce, to affirm is to negate; the problem is how not to let any of these moments crystallize into a position or a program via the fetishism that transforms relations into objects. Class analysis pulls the world out of an economic struggle, while bourgeois analysis attacks those struggles as reinforcing workers' identity. The identity politics of whiteness performs a very similar maneuver when it attacks liberation politics undertaken by marginalized groups as "divisive"—in other words, "reductive." Right-wing and authoritarian effects tend to flow from this position whatever the context, with some of the dangerous absurdities on display in the current German culture wars a good indication.

Perhaps the motif that moves through all these has something to do with scale. Scale is immanently connected to political and artistic strategy, to deciding how to situate an action or an inquiry. Reduction is about scale. But it is also about site. A kind of displacement needs to happen in order bring something to visibility, from inactuality to actuality. The use of "real" objects as citations in artwork, when artwork cites from reality even as it constitutes an inflected or diagonal reality to the referent, is an instance of the strategy. It's one that Budor deploys when she shrinks the grand rooms of the palazzo by wedging assembly-line tables into them—a class struggle of scale, unmediated by narrative or the emollient of heritage. Long after the strikes of the *tabacchine*, the machines they abandoned have claimed the bosses' palaces. These sinuous behemoths, now stuck at the "halt" setting of their Fascist-vintage martial controls (the machine could either "halt" or "march"), radiate the power of reduction as an artifact of the wrong place and the out-of-scale, just as the achievement of autoreduction was a high-water mark of working-class power weakness—the inability to pay.

The machines have been quiet for some time, and several decades have also elapsed since gaps in purchasing power have been dealt with through the force of collective refusal. The power of money has reasserted itself, which has also had the effect of placing limits on the critical traction of art's displacement strategies as hard as those that the walls of the Progetto place on the tobacco tables. Casting critique as unmediated transit between a way of seeing and actual change in the world, however, would be a self-imposed limit of another kind. Artwork's power comes not just from its ability to deftly cite a parallel reality but from its offer of the alternate logic that would obtain there. I've been suggesting that reduction is the starting point of transformation, the gamble that constitutes refusal or withdrawal; reduction as revolt in logic and in praxis. Transposing this idea into the register of an artwork shifts the problem into one of scale and placement. The disjunction between the clarity of the encounter and its insertion into uncertain value circuits is great. Materiality is in fact a very forceful demonstration, but its meaning varies according to the time in which it exists as well as the times it can evoke. The machine that brought you here will not be the same machine that takes you home.

1 Fredric Jameson, "World Reduction in Le Guin: The Emergence of Utopian Narrative," *Science Fiction Studies* 2, no. 3 (November 1975): 221–30.

2 Jacques Rancière, "Préface," in Pierre-Simon Ballanche, *Première Sécession de la plebe*, 22. Quoted in Jussi Pamussari, "Philosophers Don't Spring Up Like Mushrooms: On Rancière's Heretic Method," afterword to Rancière, *Marx in the Woods: The Dialectic of Reason and Private Interest*, trans. Pamussari (Helsinki: Rab-Rab Press, 2019), 48.

3 Beverley Best, "Distilling a Value Theory of Ideology from Volume Three of *Capital*," *Historical Materialism* 23, no. 3 (September 2015), 101–41.

4 Claire Fontaine, *Human Strike Has Already Begun and Other Writings* (Berlin: Mute; Lüneberg, Germany: Post-Media Lab, Leuphana University, 2013).

Autoreduction

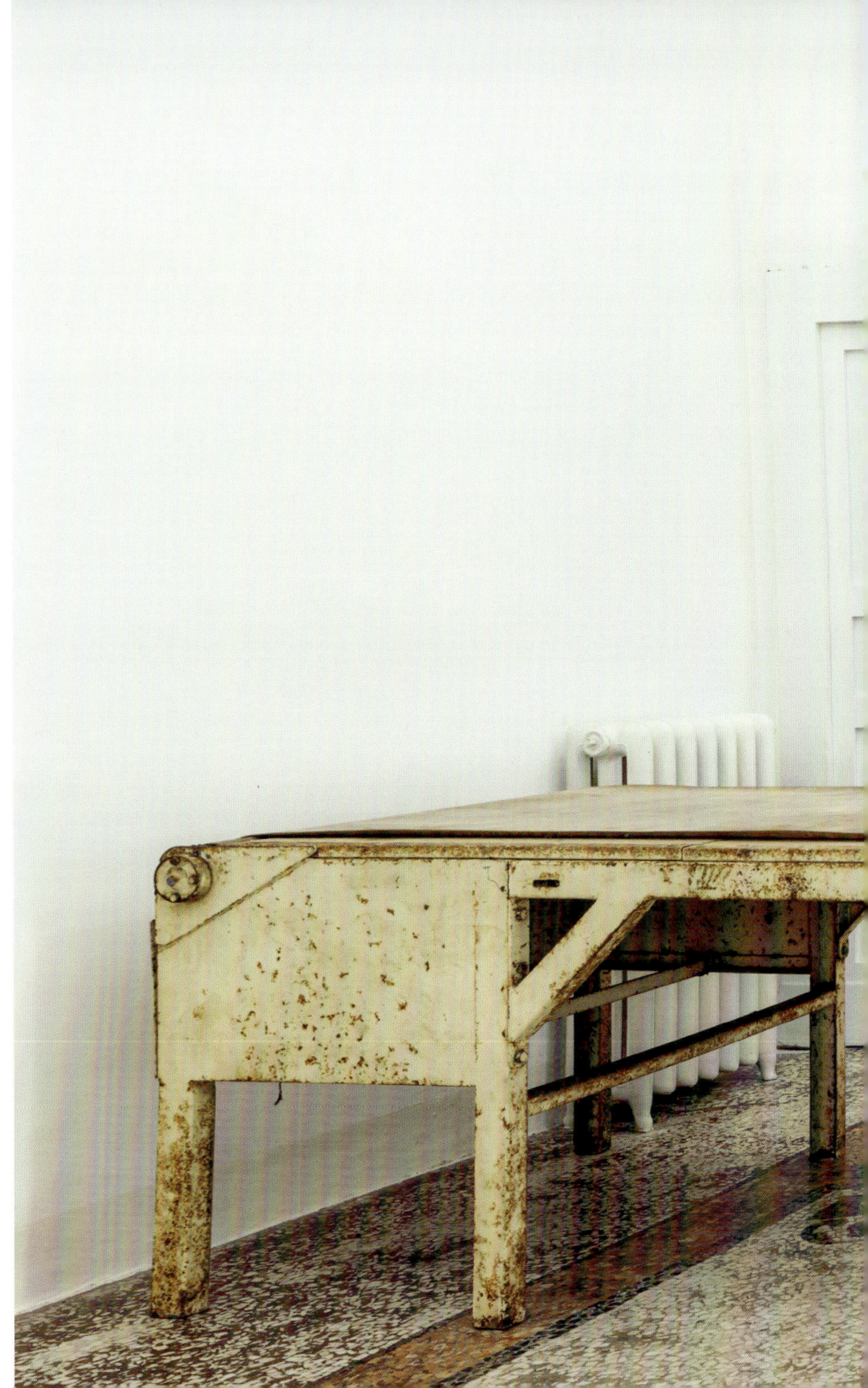

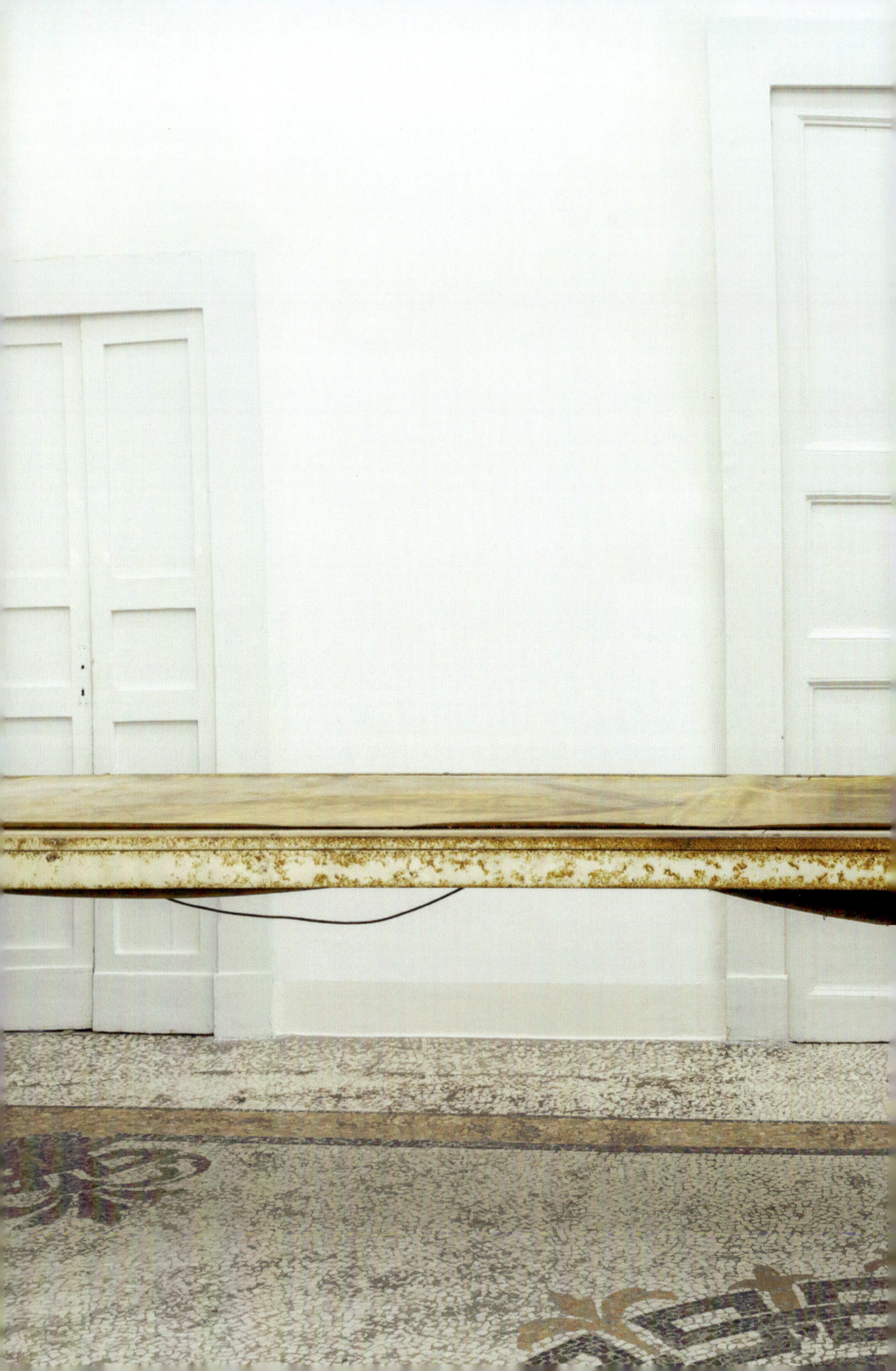

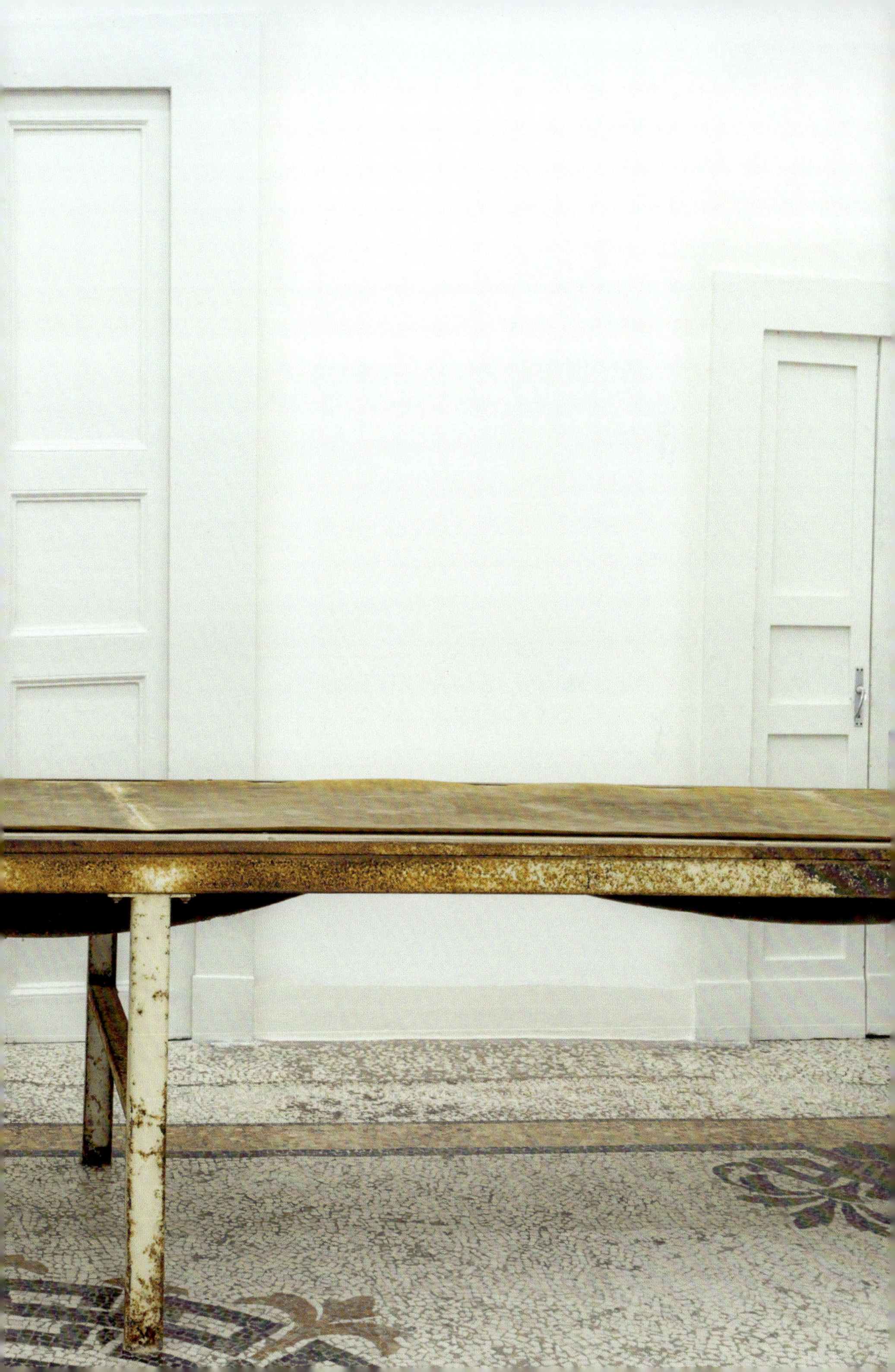

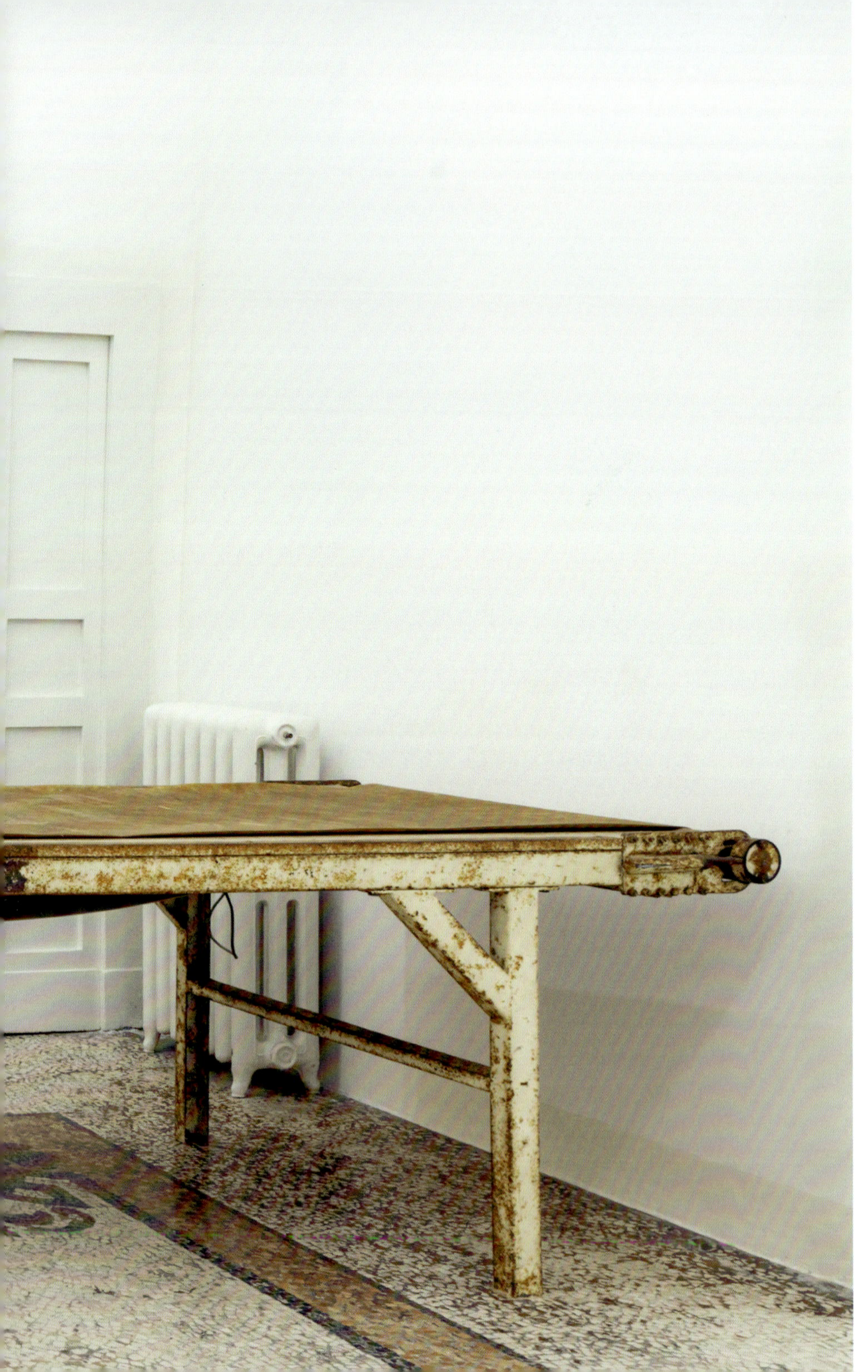

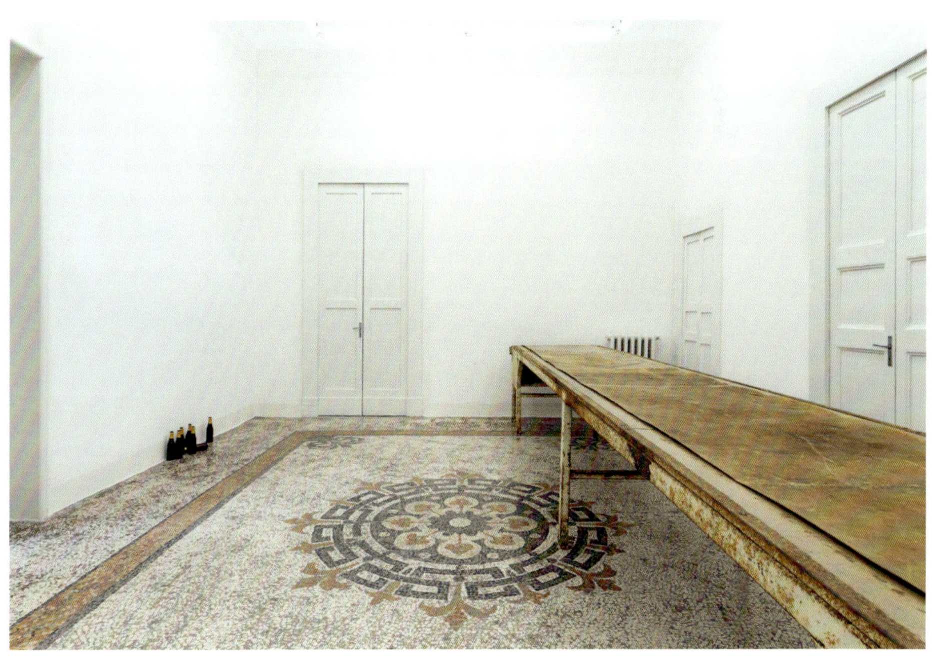

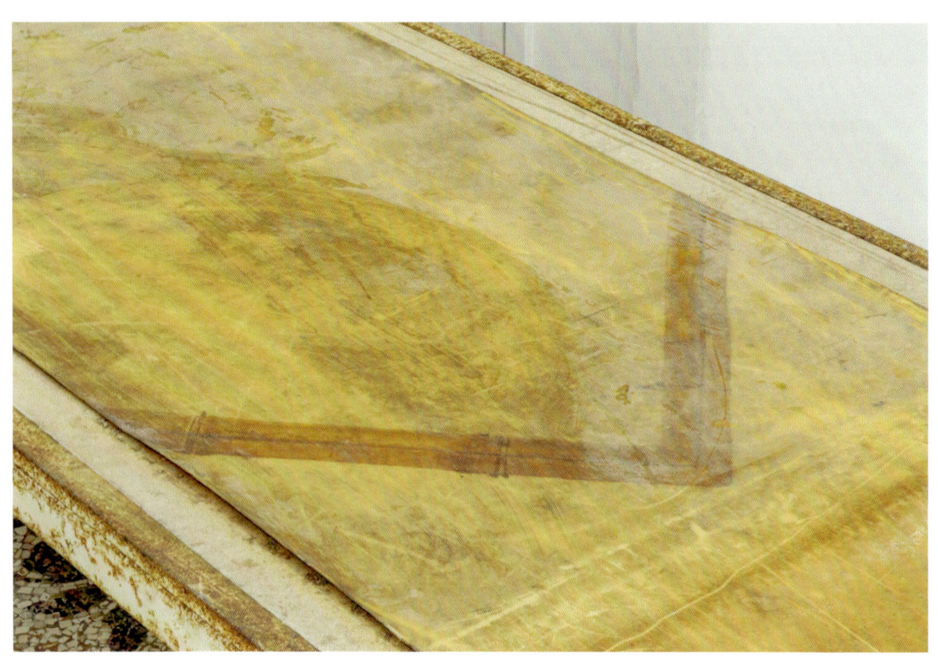

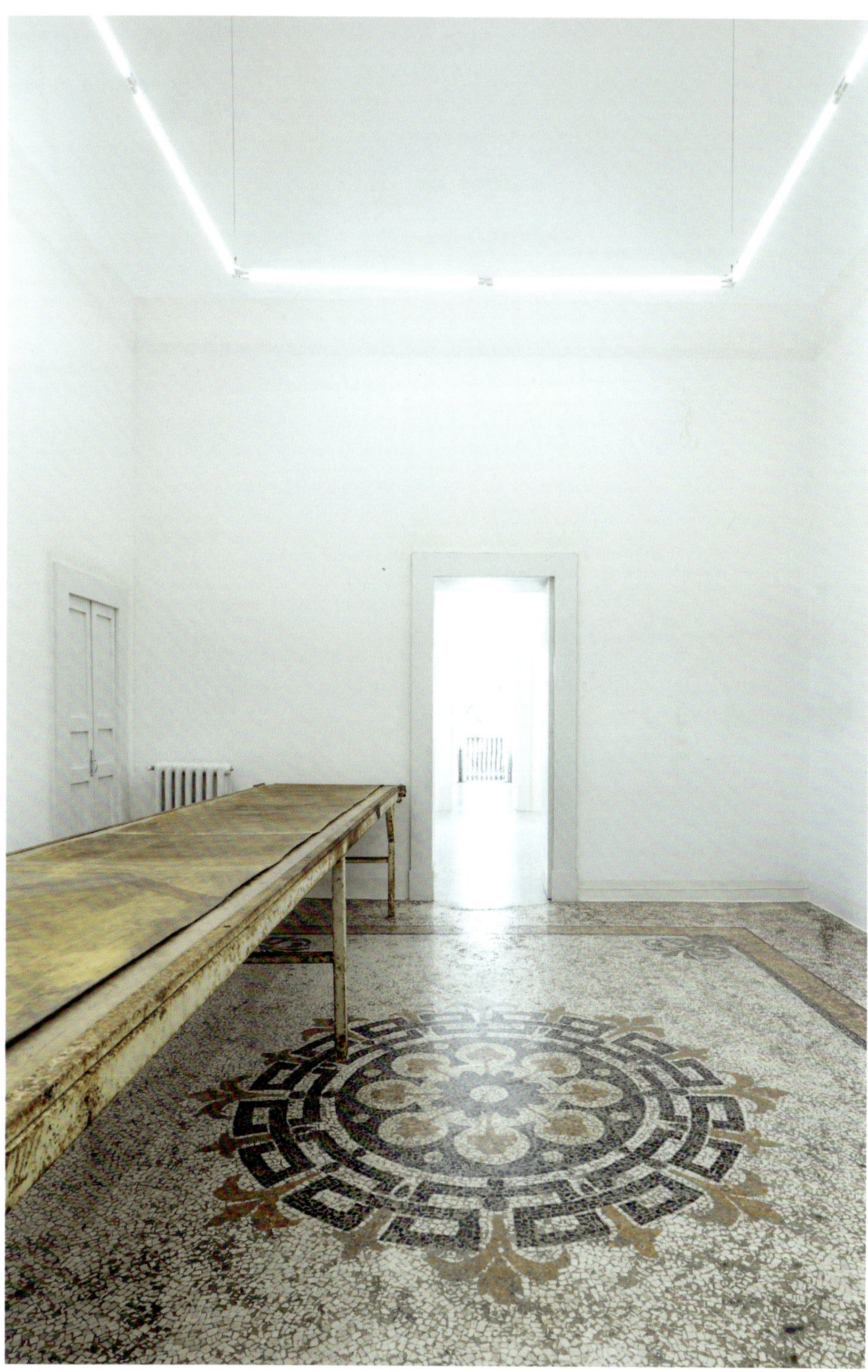

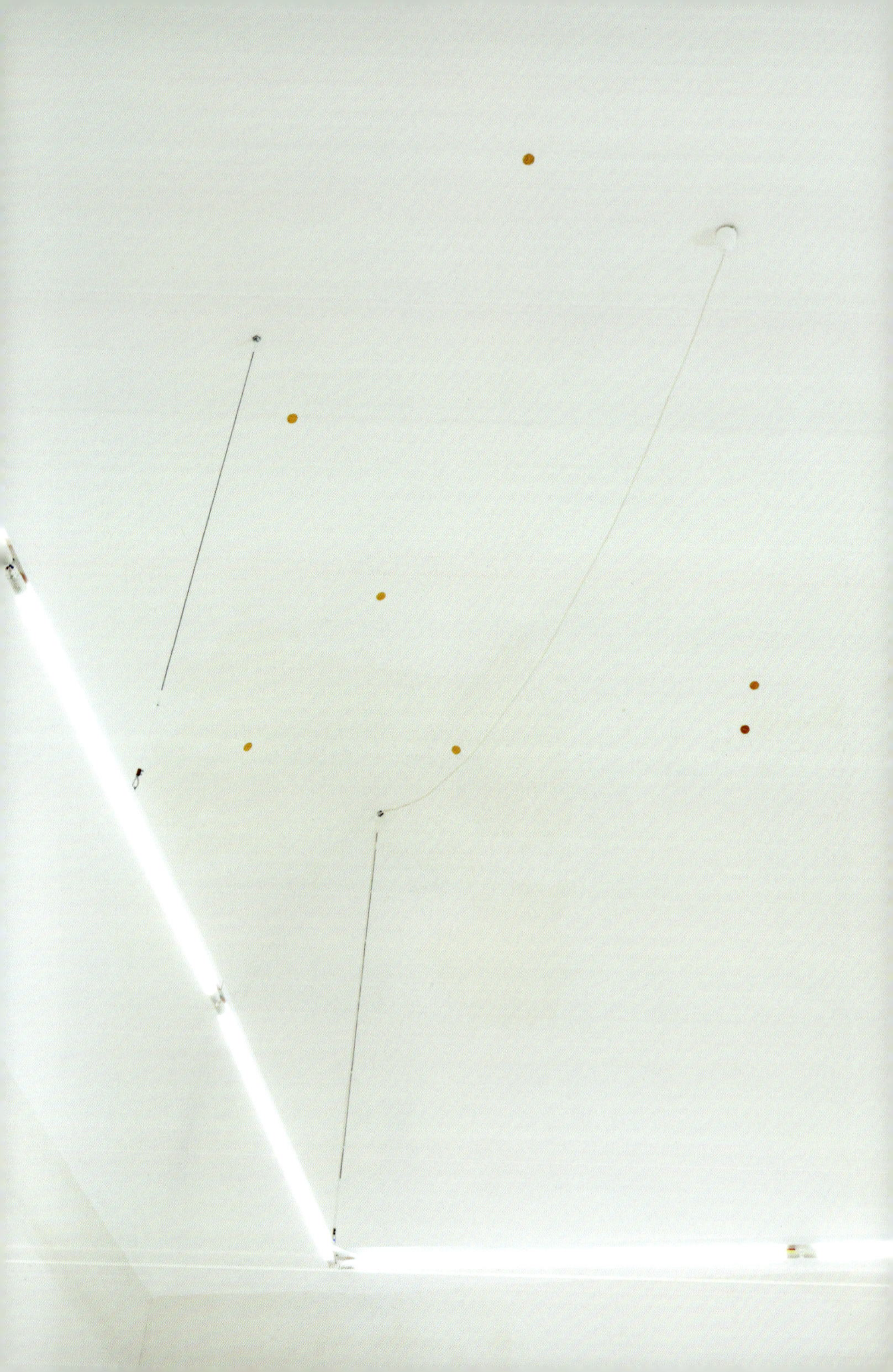

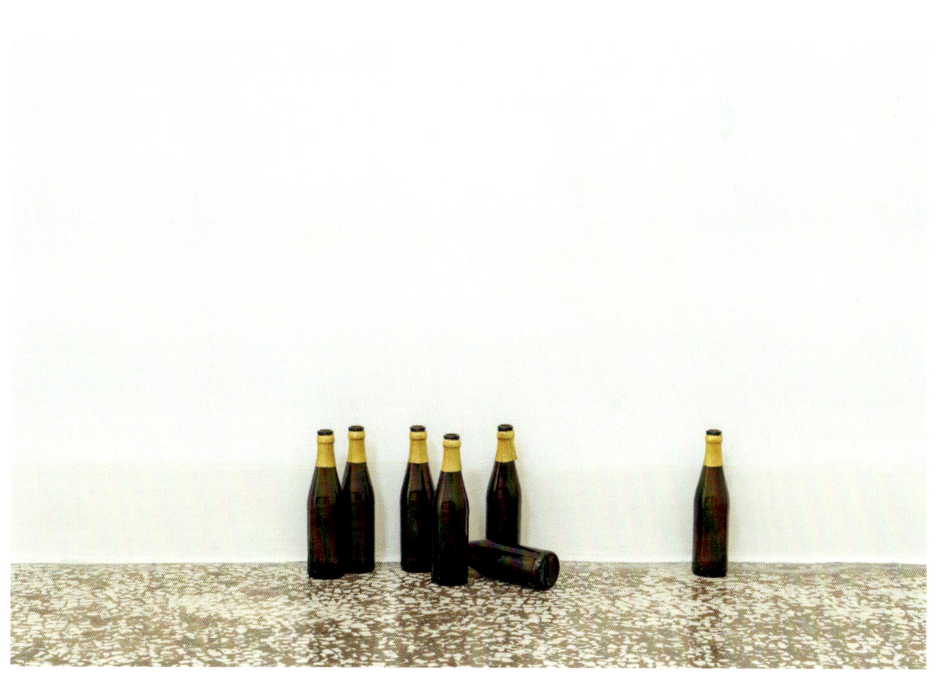

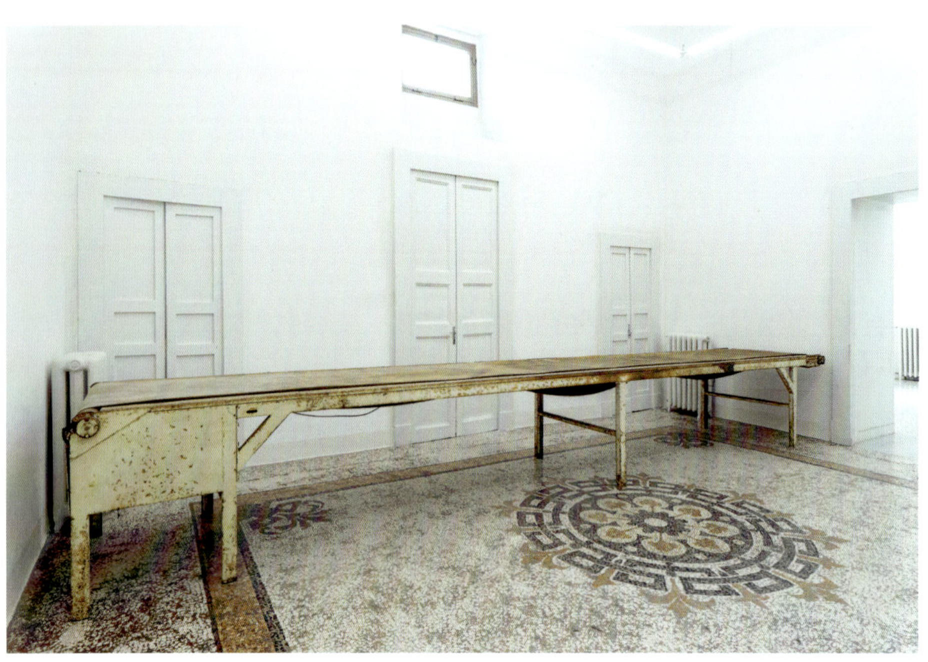

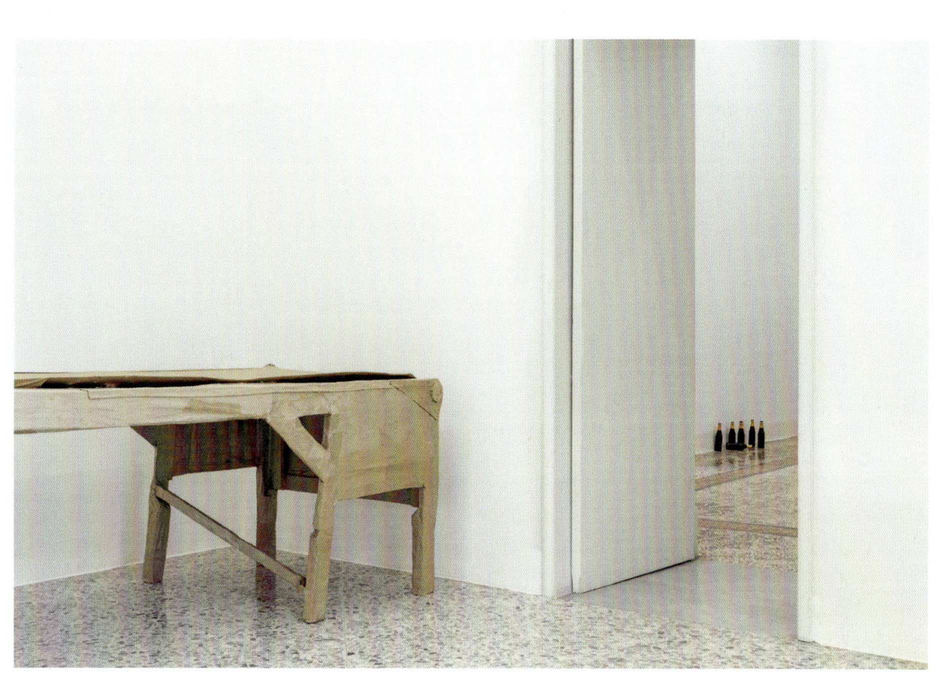

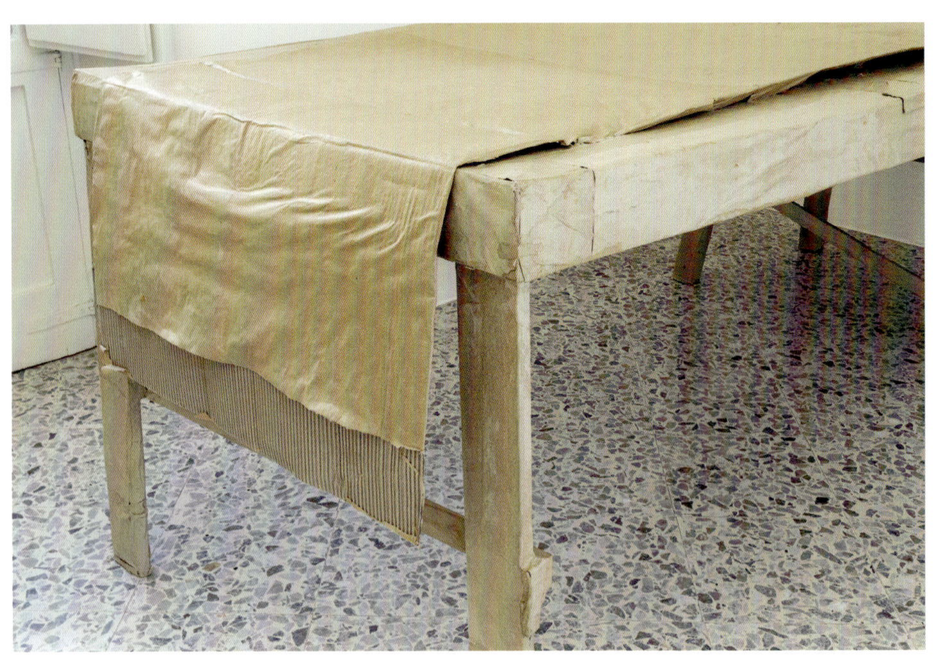

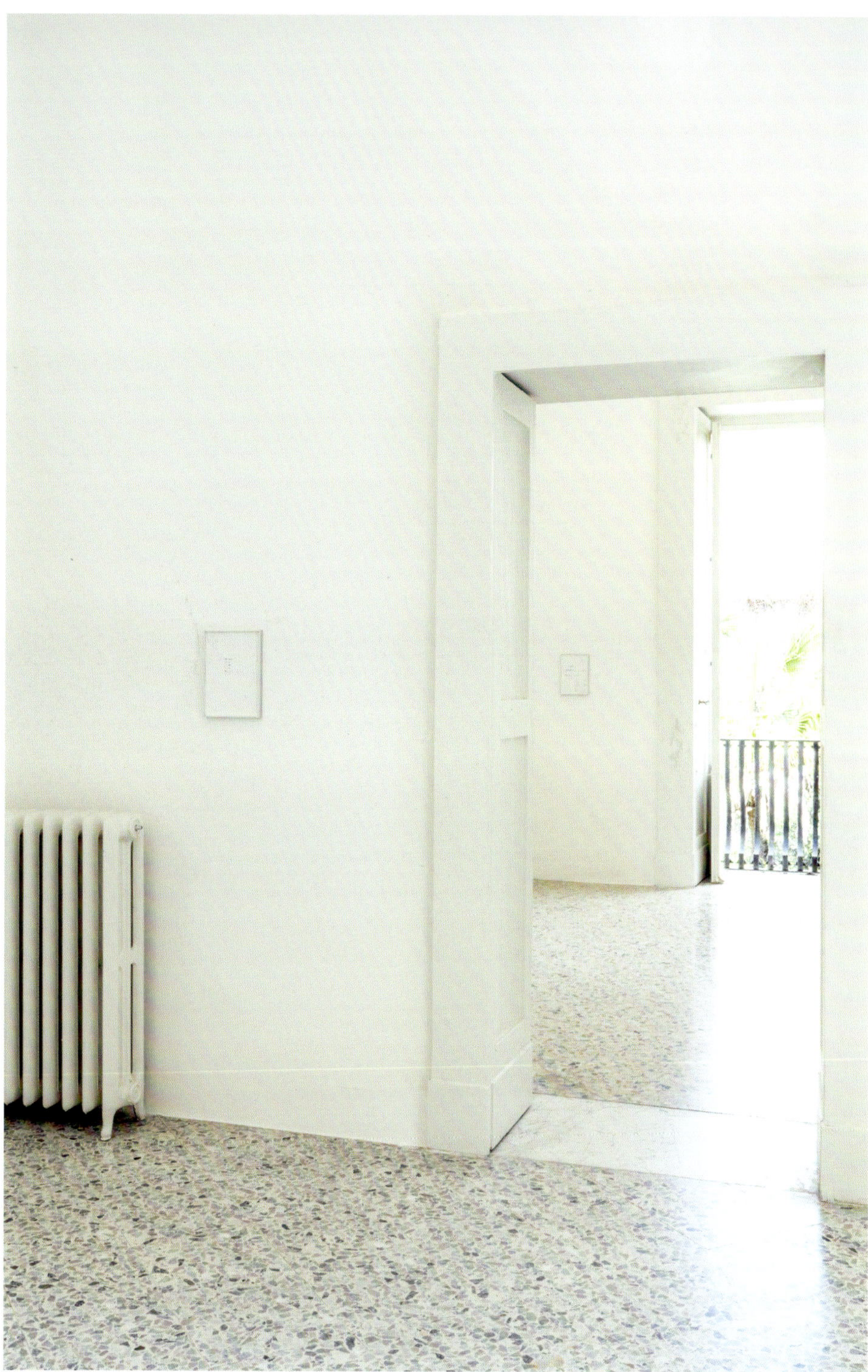

NOT Long
NOT you
NOT GOOD
not NOW
NOT Personal
NOT over

ANNOTAZIONE
Auto - Descrizione
le Terrazze sono SENZA Regolamento E Non sufficienti .
Lo SCOPERTO ANTICIPATO NON è una vocazione MA un' Operazione .

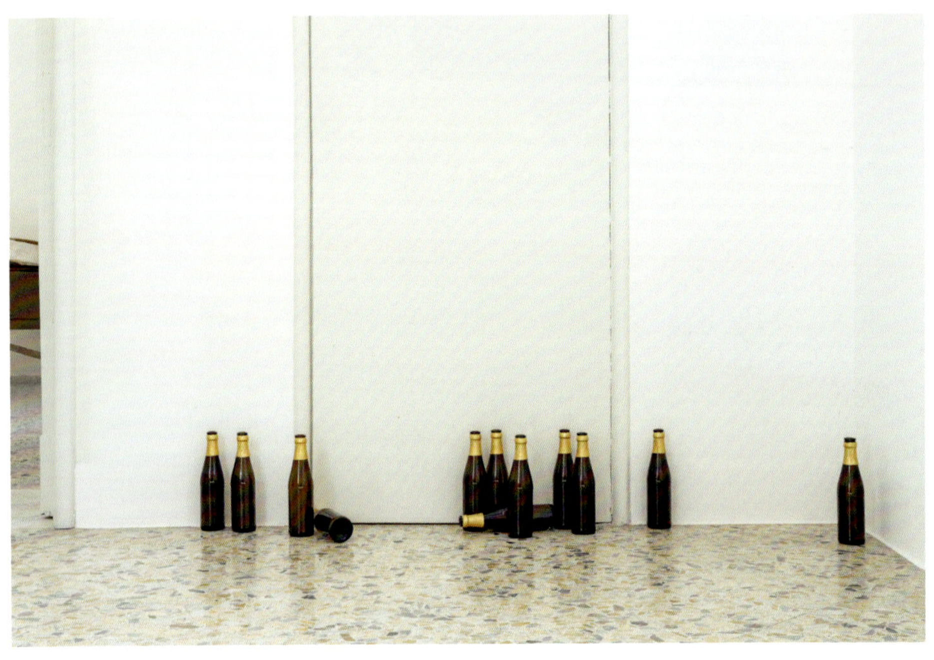

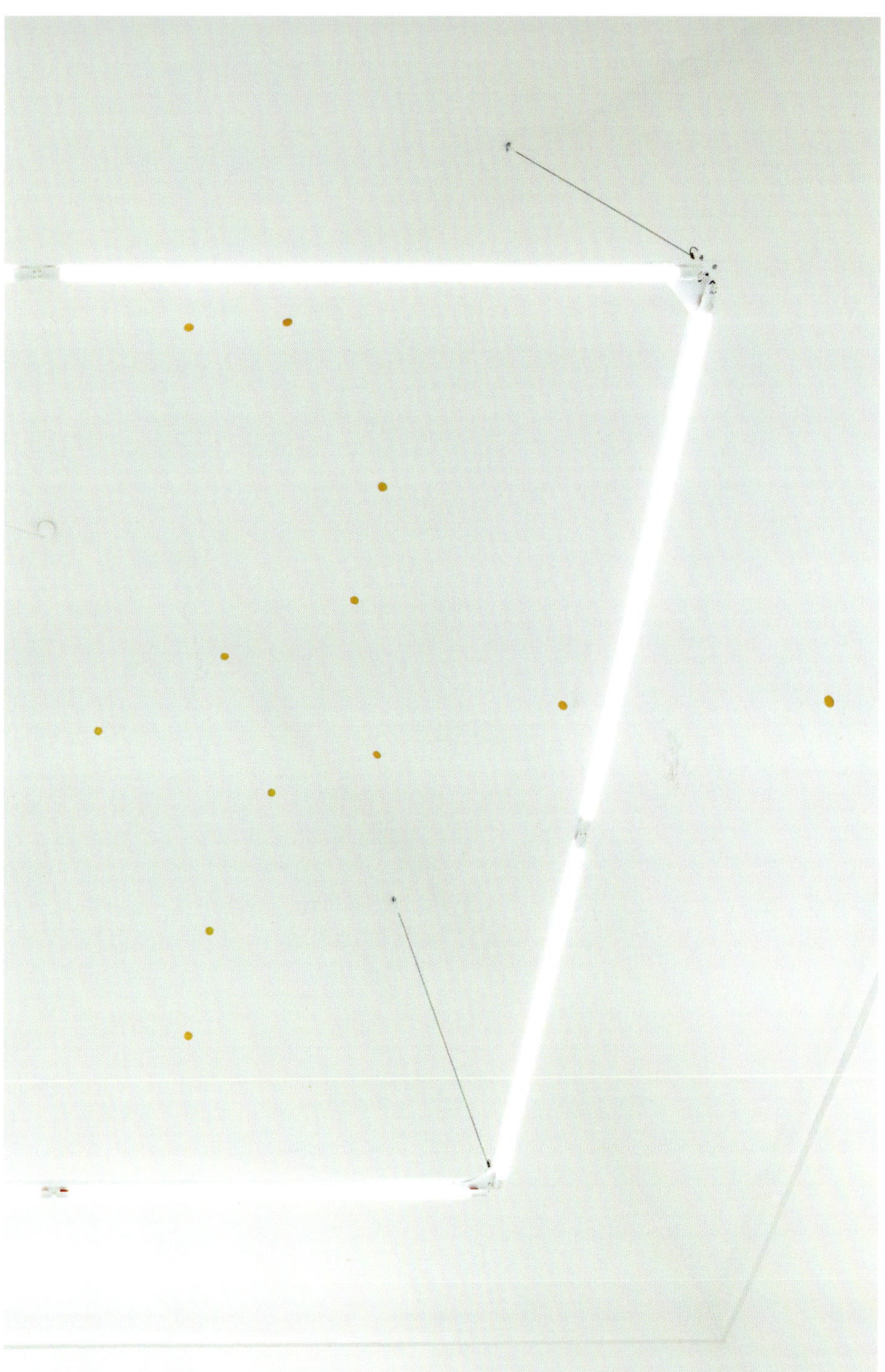

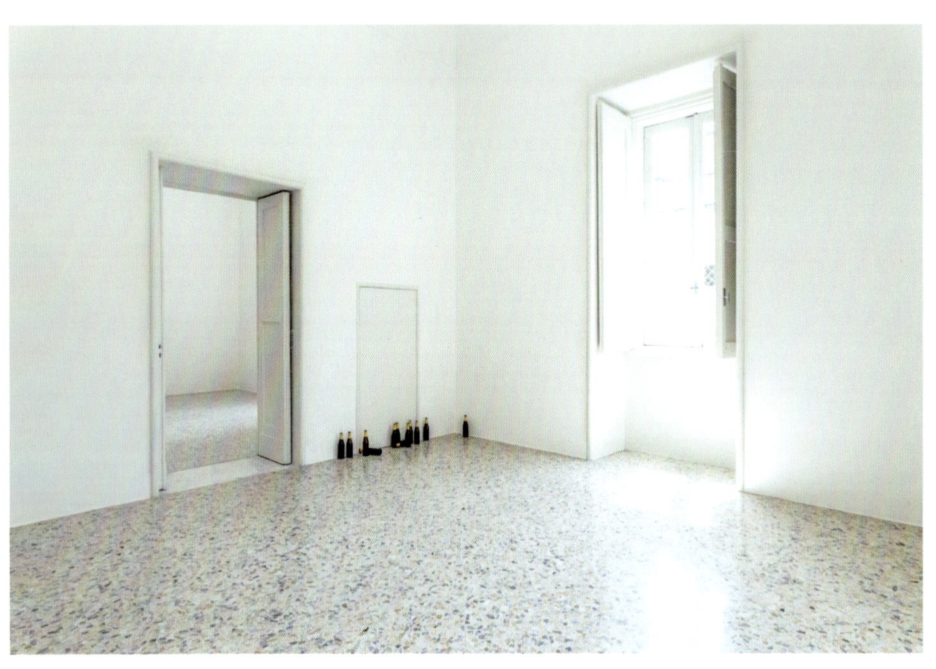

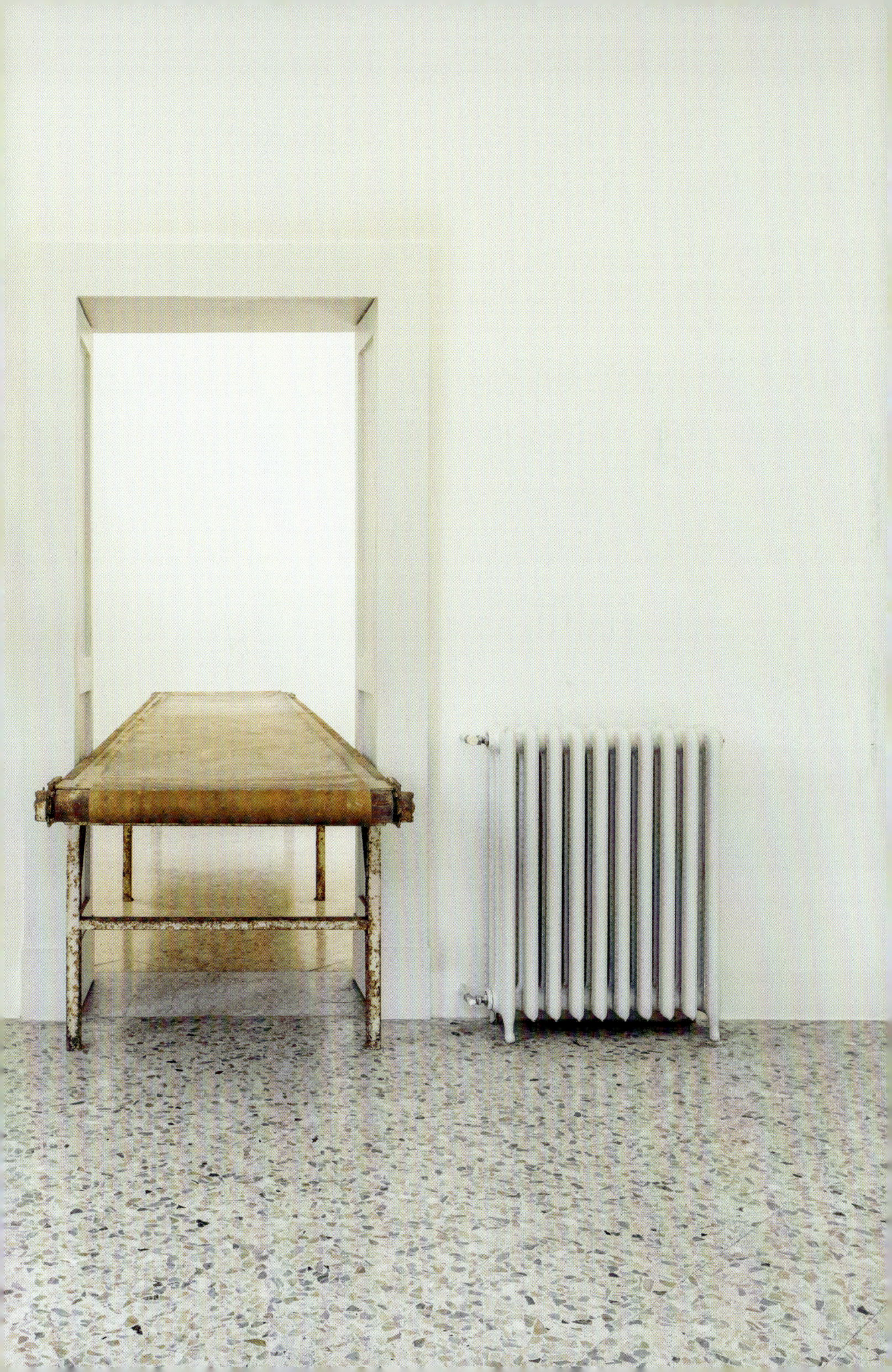

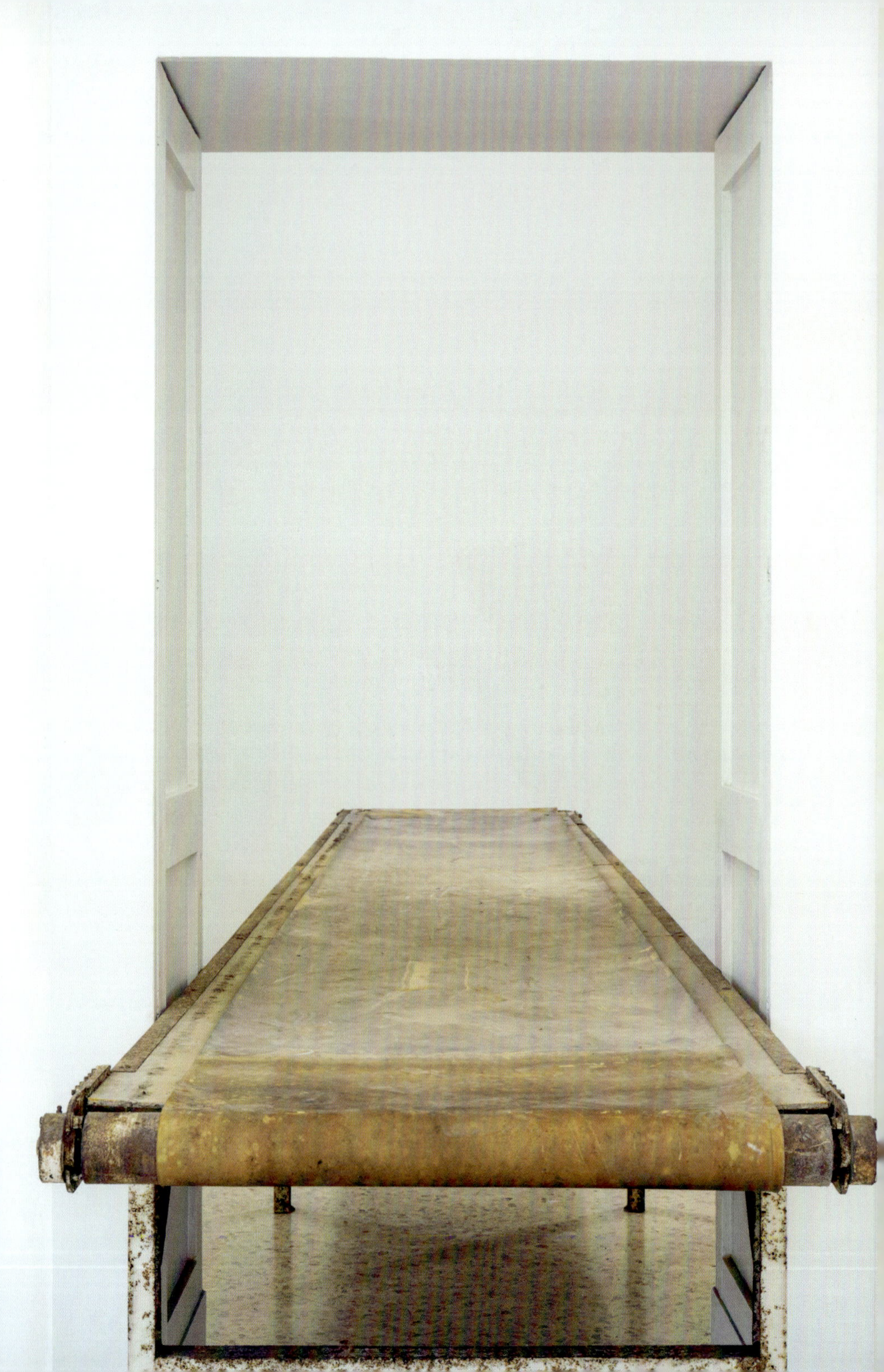

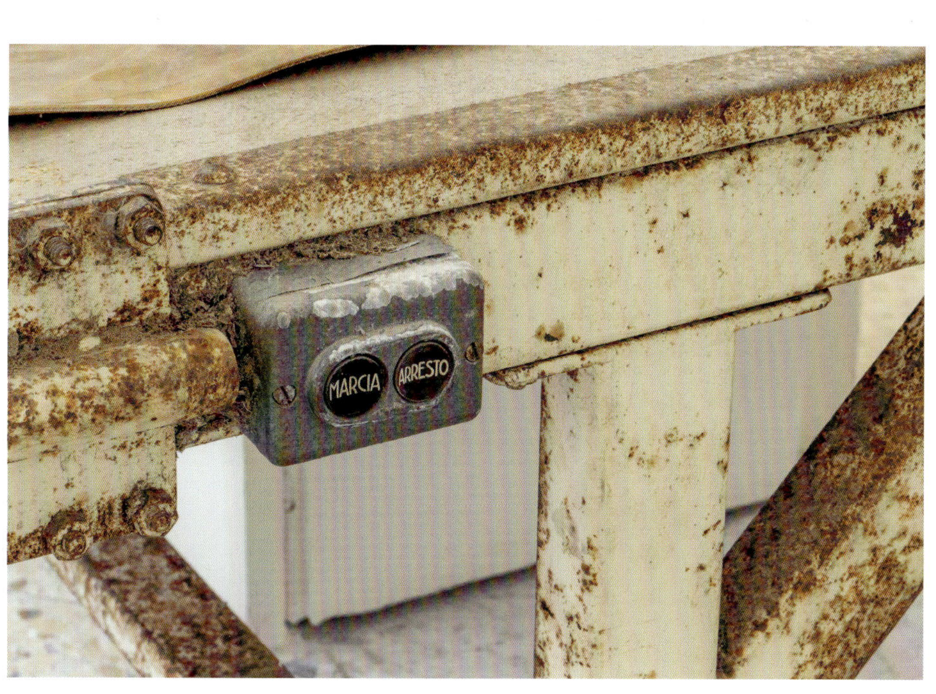
MARCIA
ARRESTO

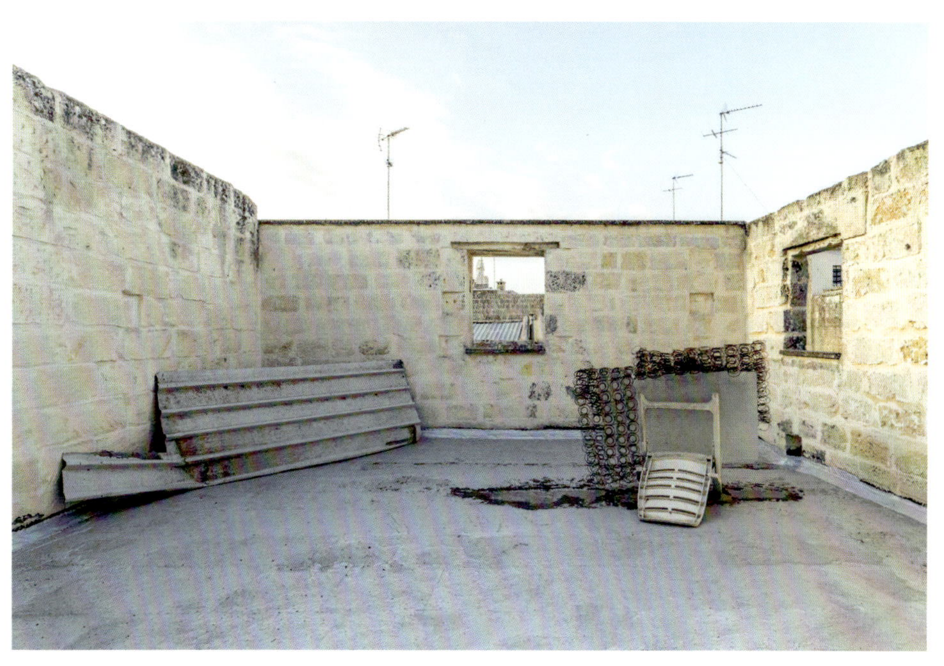

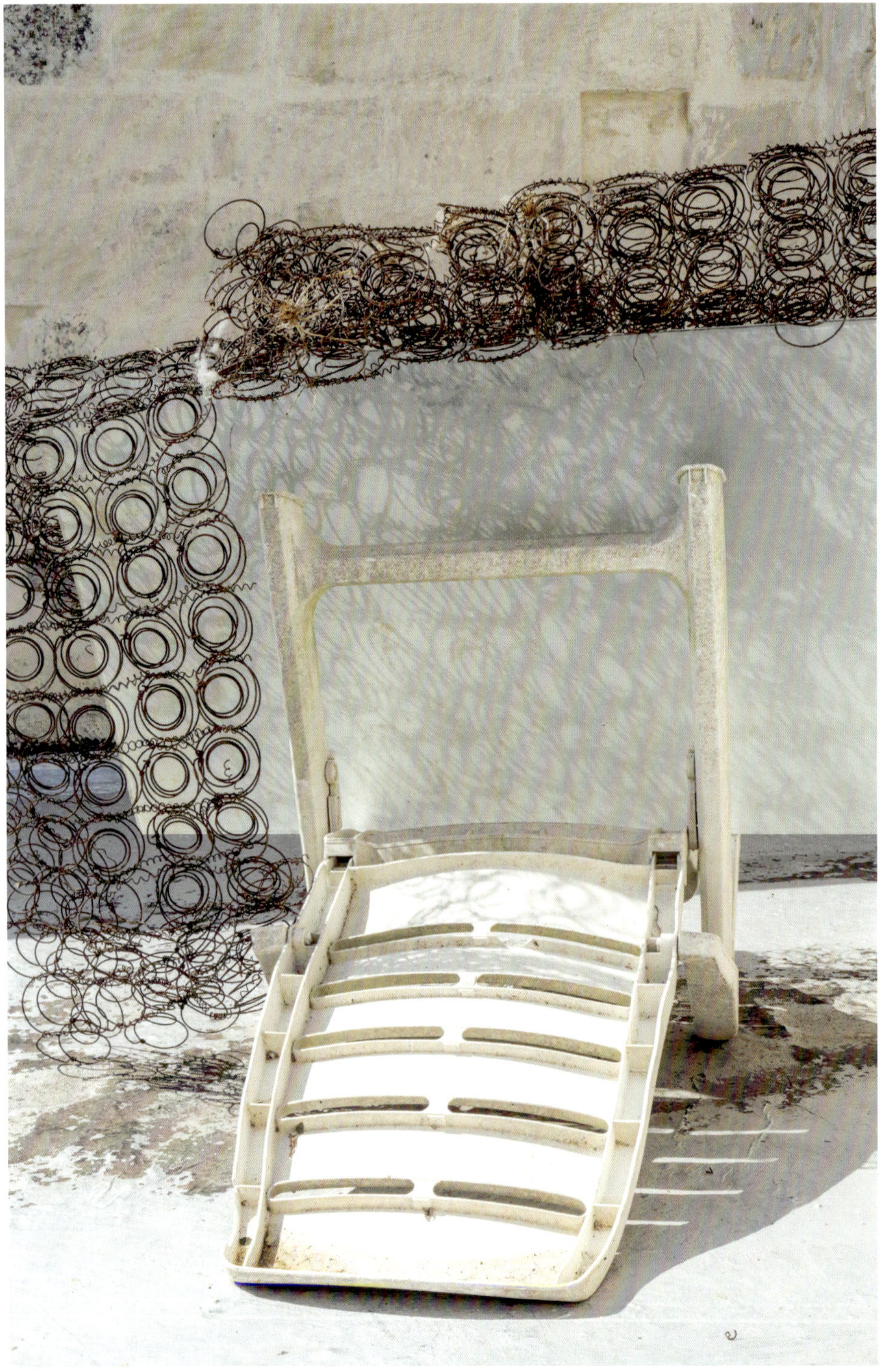

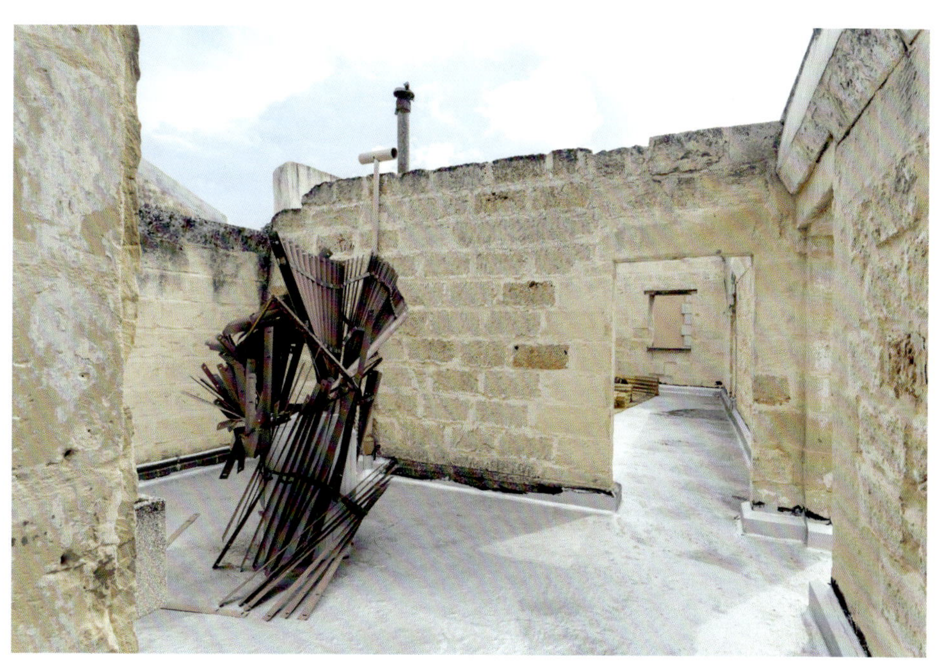

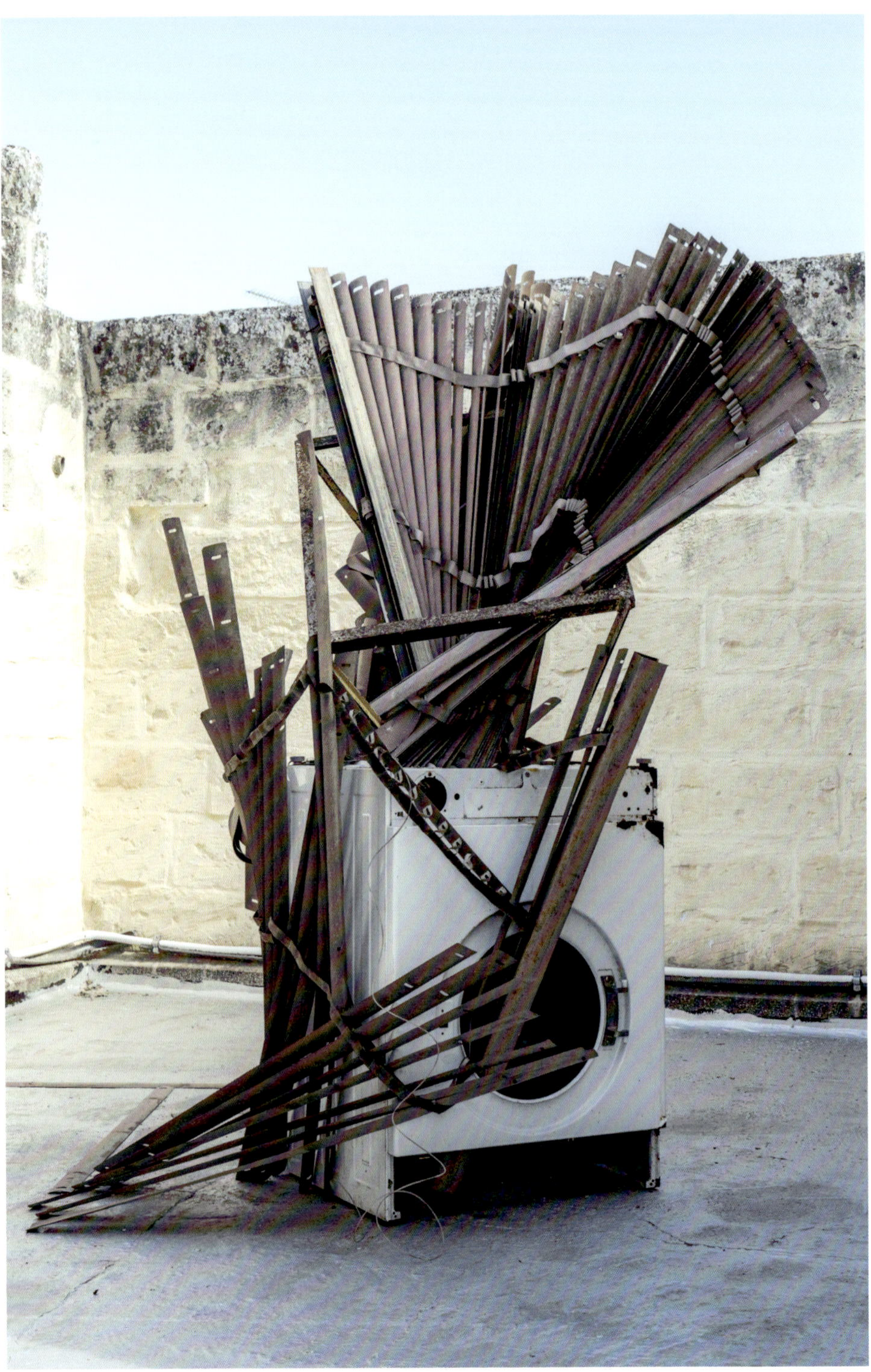

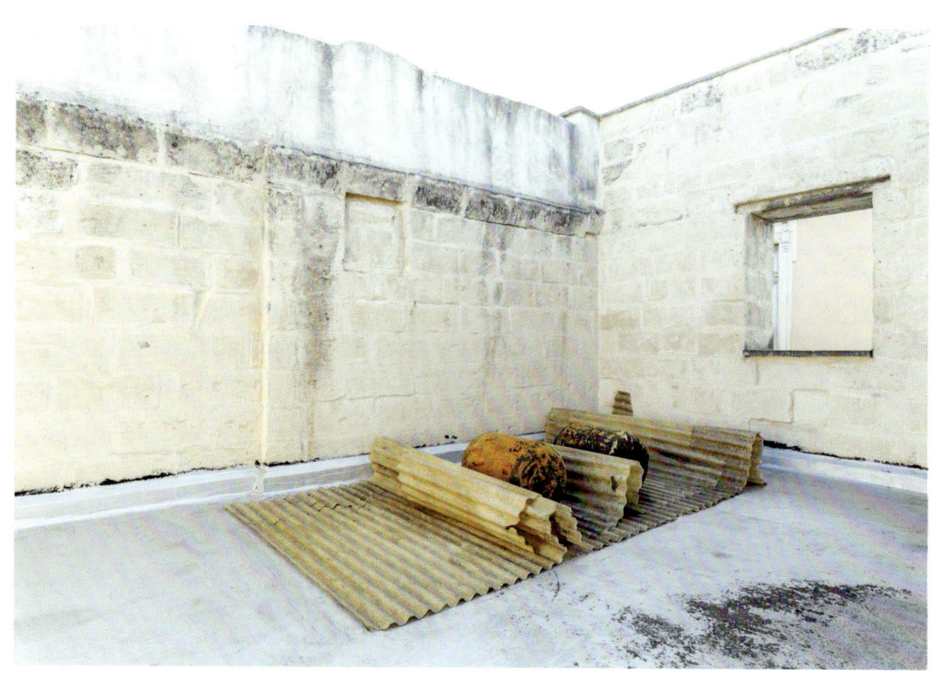

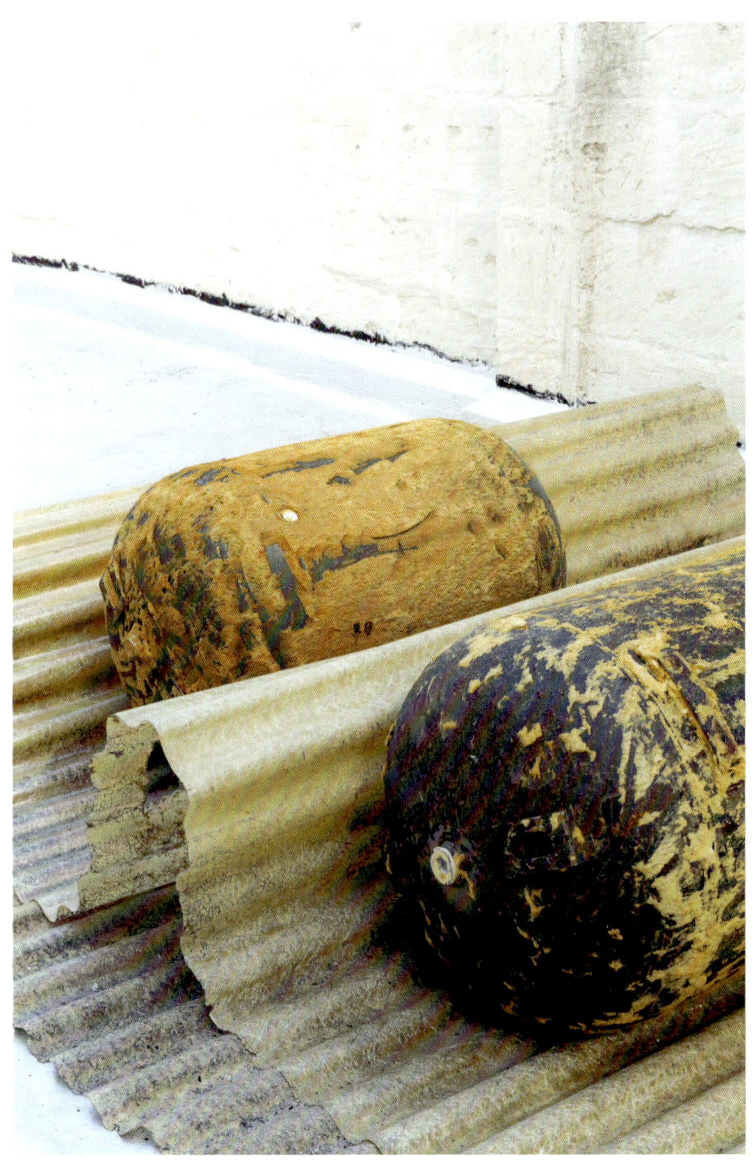

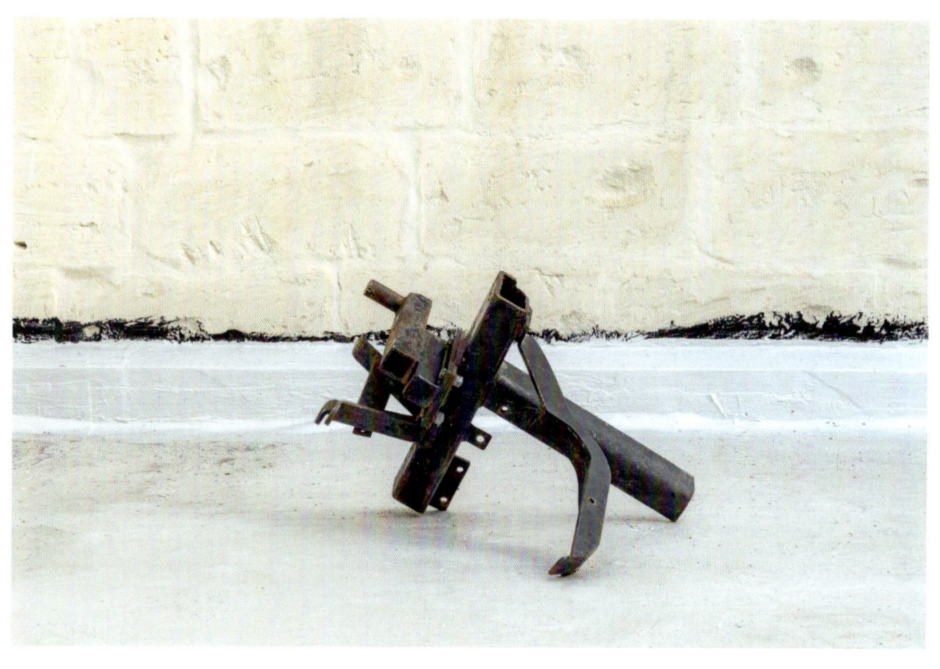

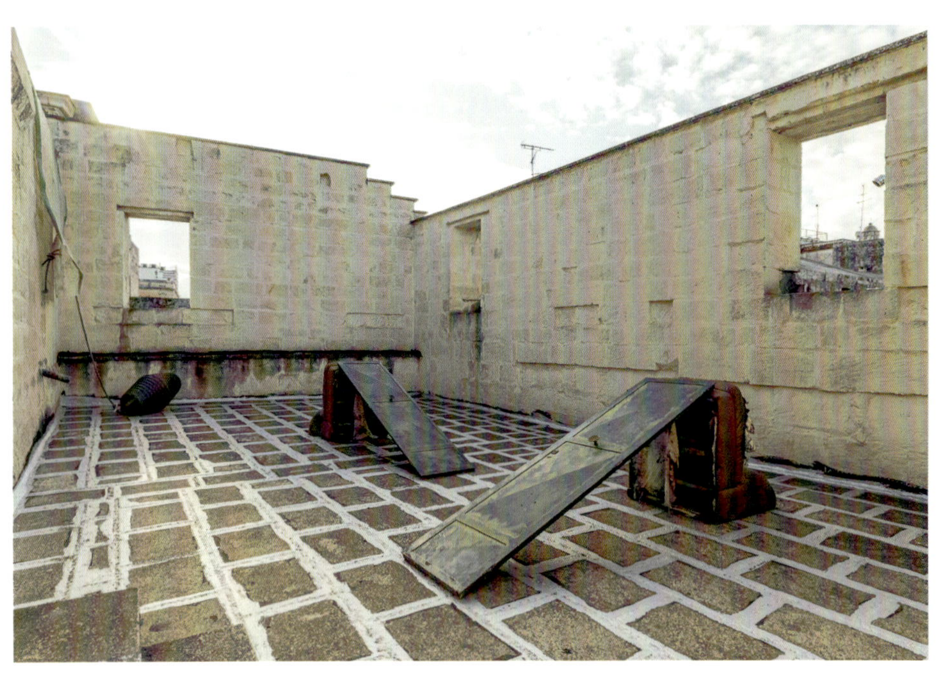

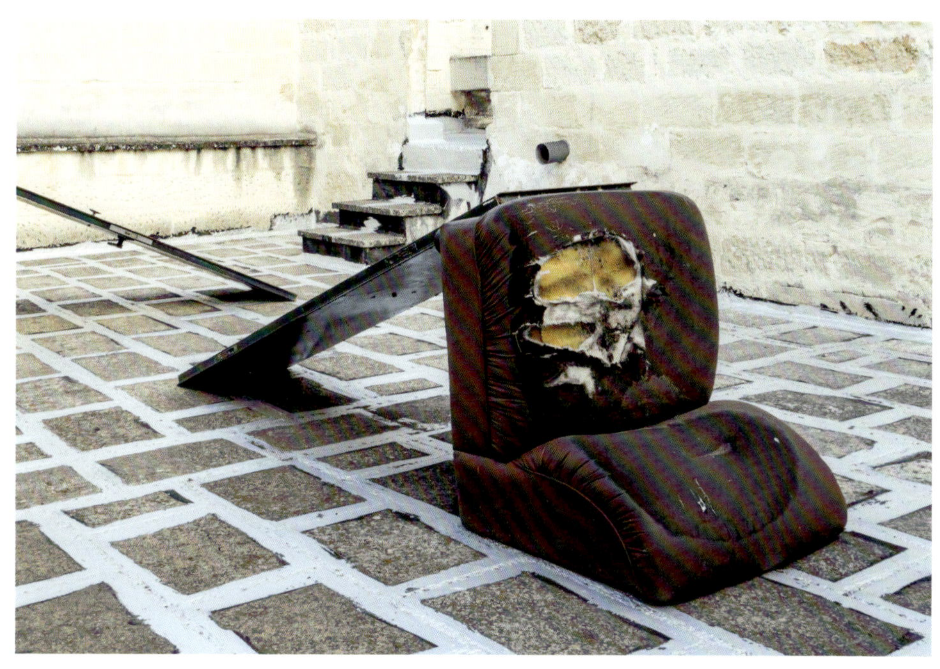

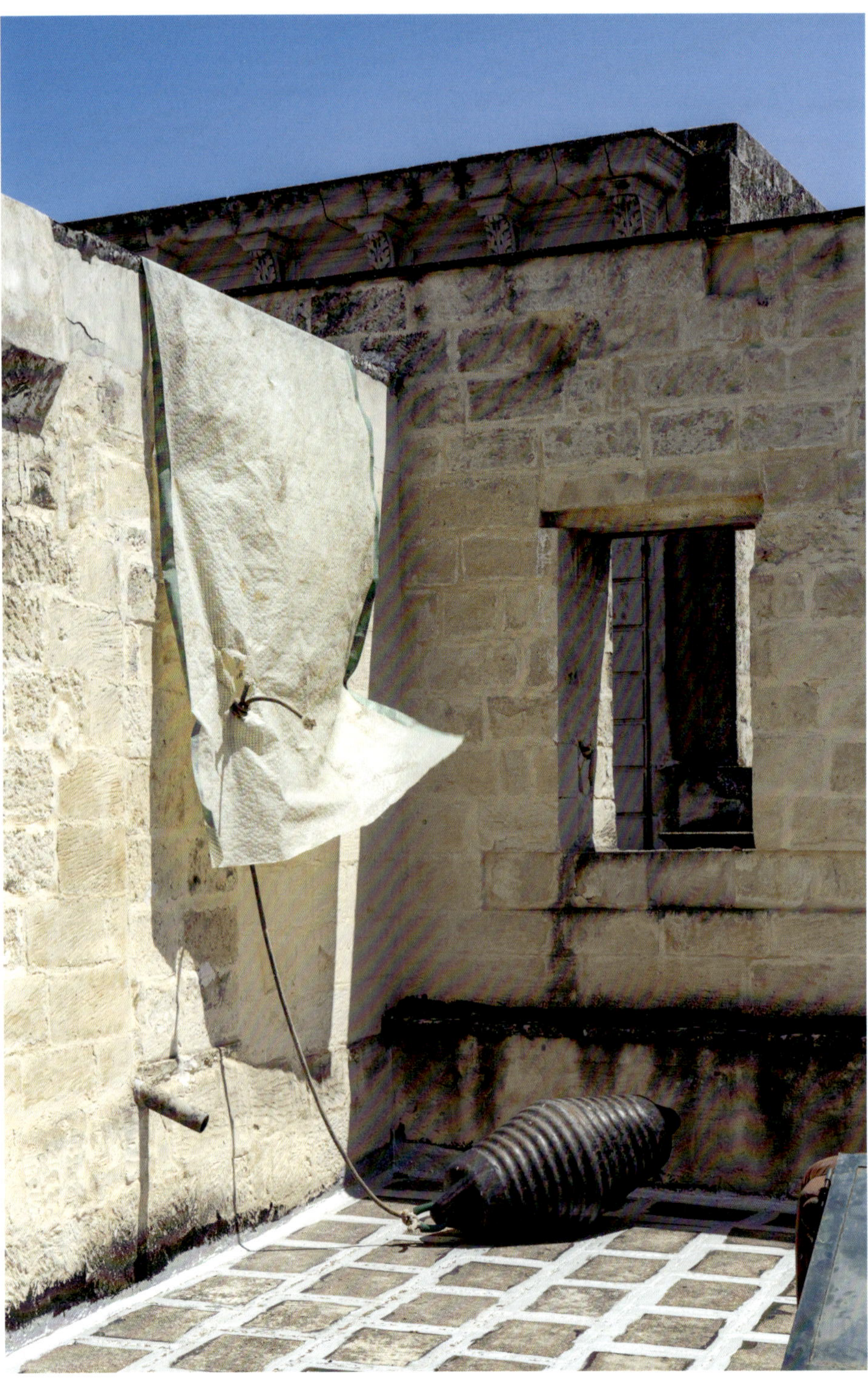

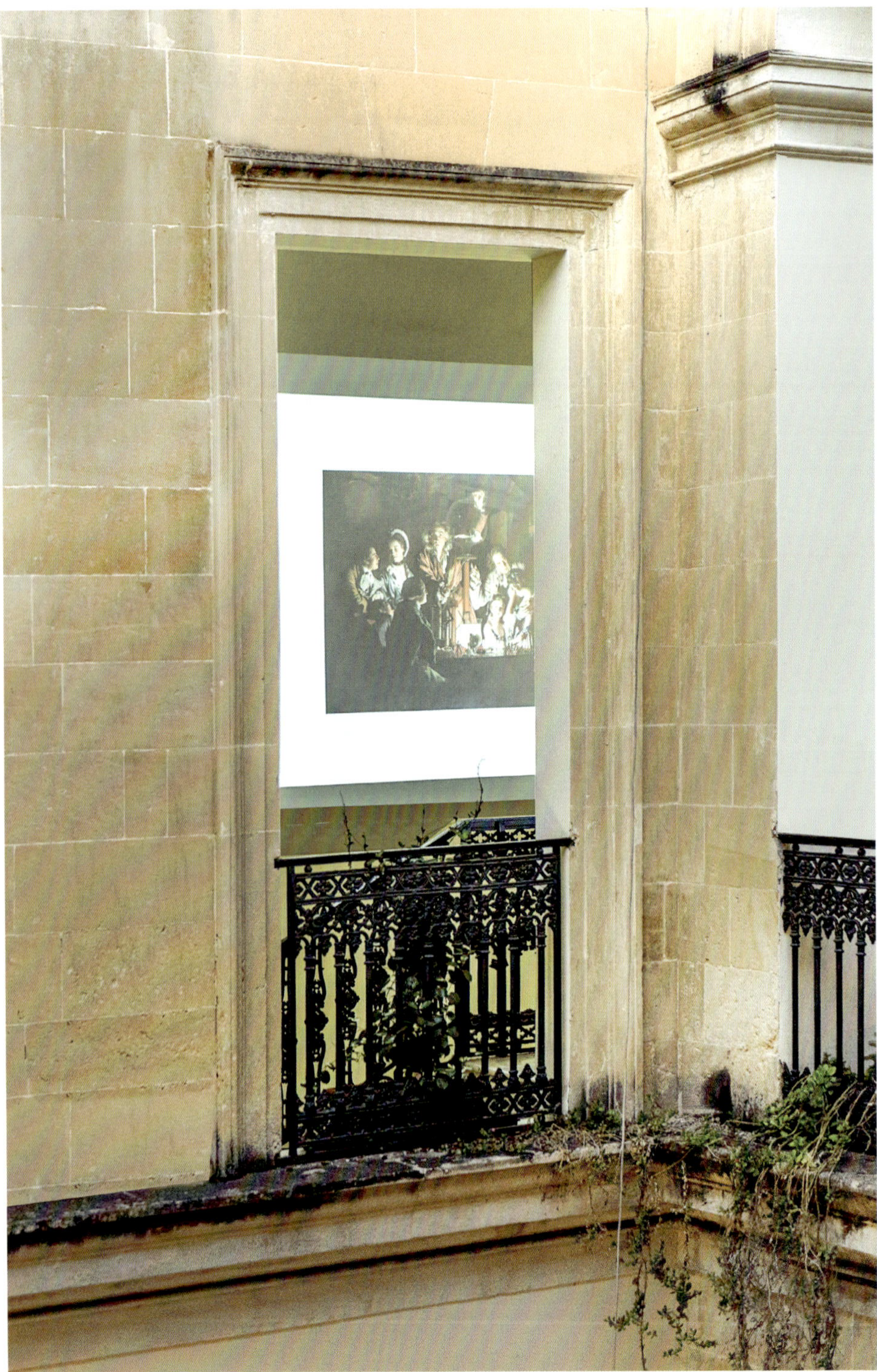

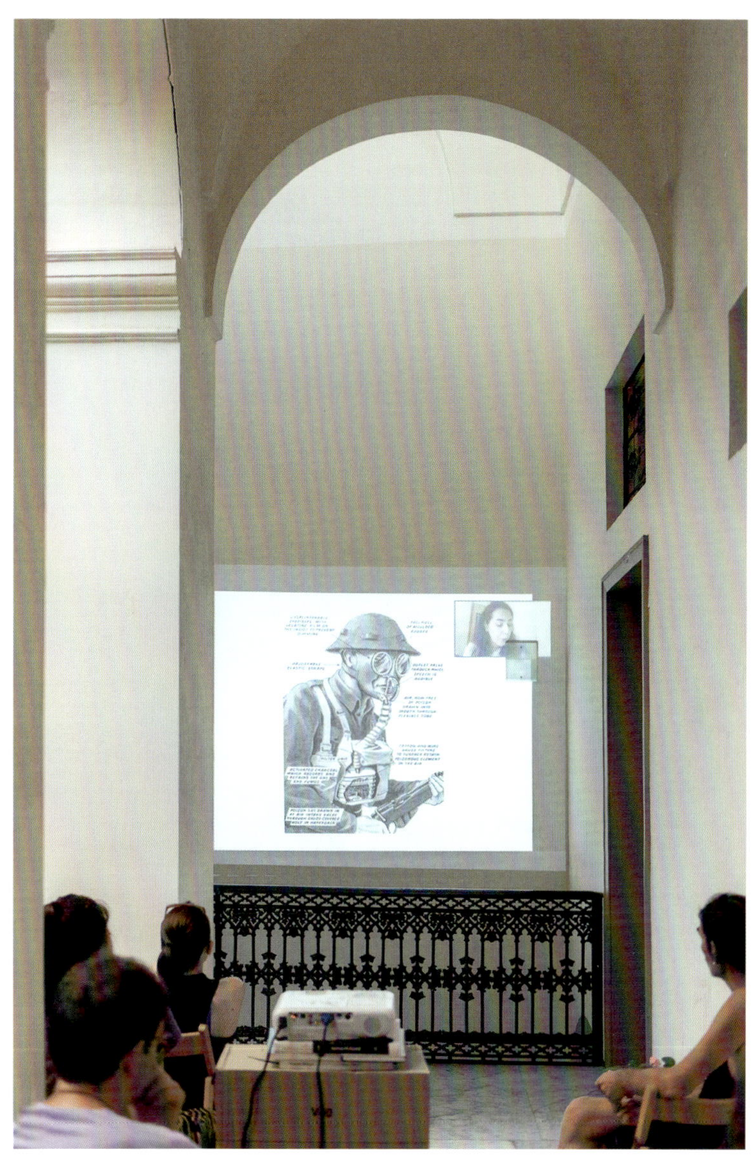

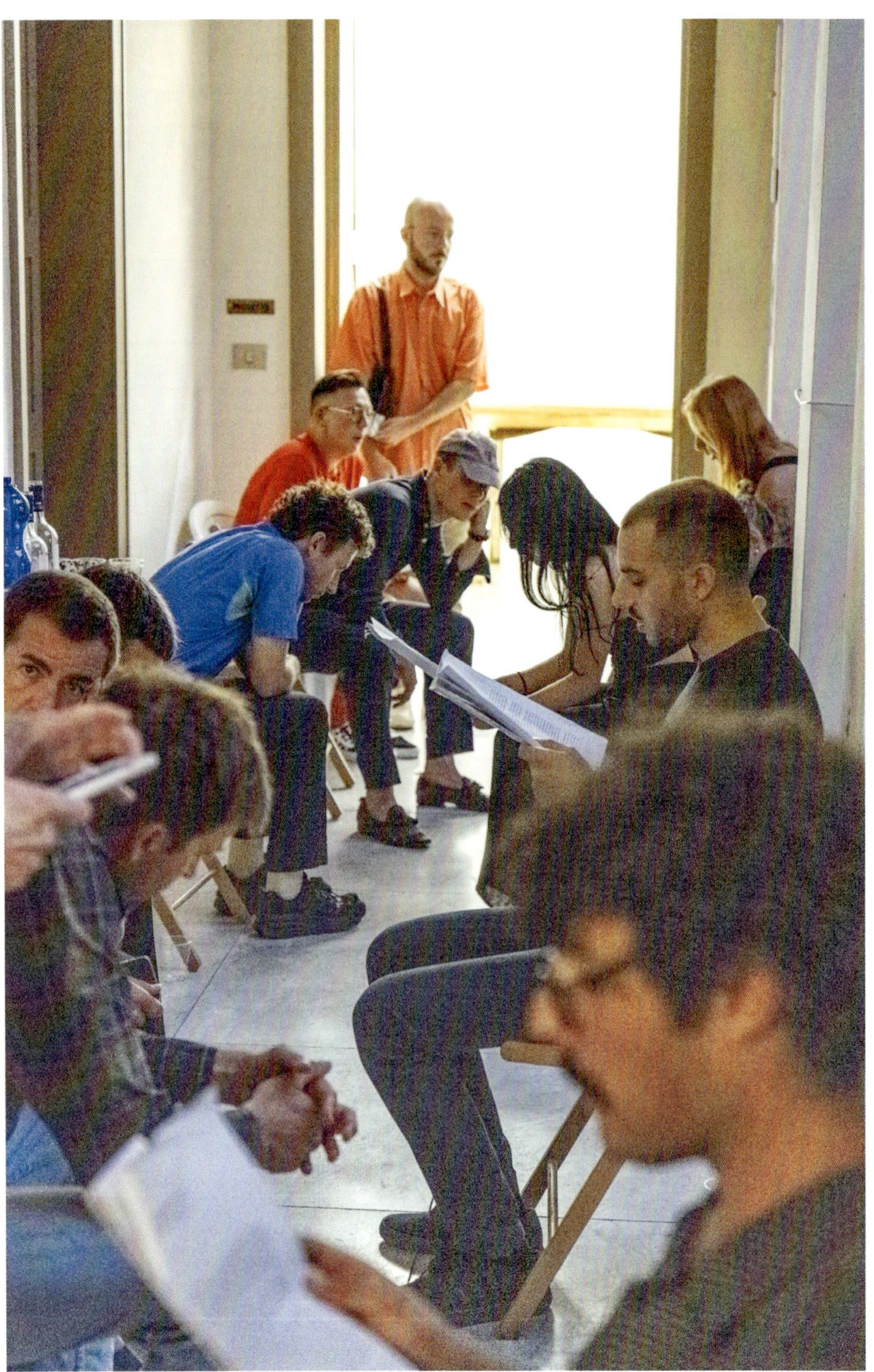

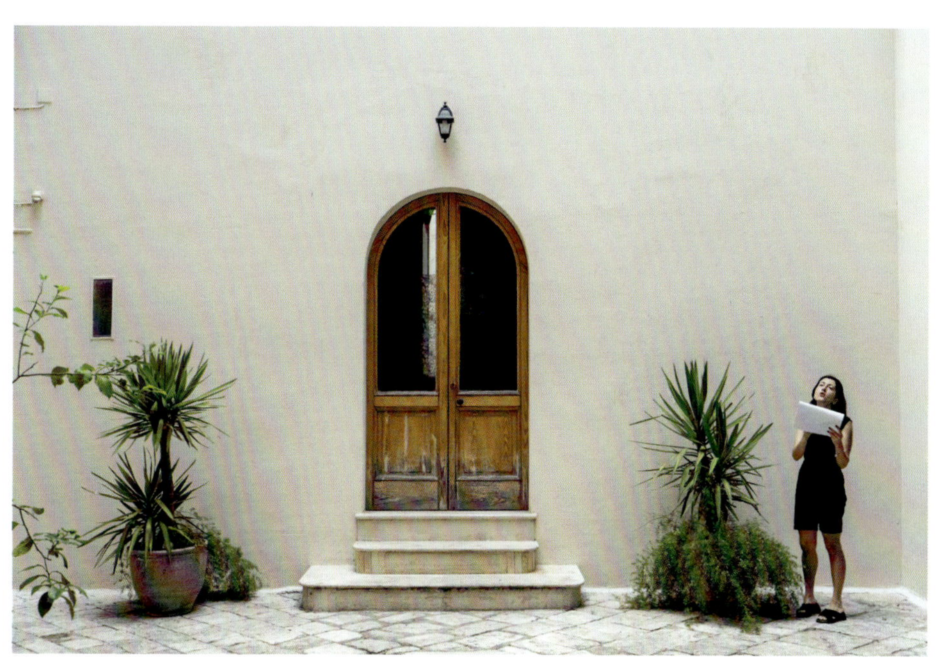

List of Works

pages 71–77 — Dora Budor
Autoreduction, exhibition views

pages 78–79 — Noah Barker
Constellation #2, 2021
Glass, aluminum

pages 80–83 — Dora Budor
Autoreduction, exhibition views

page 84 — Michèle Graf and Selina Grüter
Pocket Liner 8, 2021
Printed receipt paper and glue on graph paper
25 × 18 cm (framed)

page 85 — Michèle Graf and Selina Grüter
Pocket Liner 9, 2021
Printed receipt paper and glue on graph paper
25 × 18 cm (framed)

pages 86–88 — Noah Barker
Constellation #3, 2021
Glass, aluminum

pages 90–93 — Dora Budor
Autoreduction, exhibition views

pages 95, 97, 102 — Ser Serpas
Isn't Anything, 2021, installation views

page 96 — Ser Serpas
pale founding, from *Isn't Anything*, 2021

page 98 — Ser Serpas
tracing listicle generation toppling, from *Isn't Anything*, 2021

pages 99–100 — Ser Serpas
double embrace i, from *Isn't Anything*, 2021

page 101 — Ser Serpas
little talks by the highway, from *Isn't Anything*, 2021

page 103 — Ser Serpas
running along the doubling down on the easy, from *Isn't Anything*, 2021

page 104 — Ser Serpas
pin the bucket where one once stood, from *Isn't Anything*, 2021

pages 106–107 — Niloufar Emamifar
A Partnership for the Future, 2021
Lecture
Progetto balconies, July 9, 2021, 7:30 pm

pages 108–109 — Michèle Graf and Selina Grüter
The Besieged Courtyard (Il cortile assediato), 2021
Performed by Isabella Mongelli with Veronica Centonze, Alessio Cerfeda, Chiara Papaleo, Federico Rizzo, and Veronica Vergari
Progetto courtyard, July 19, 2021, 8 pm

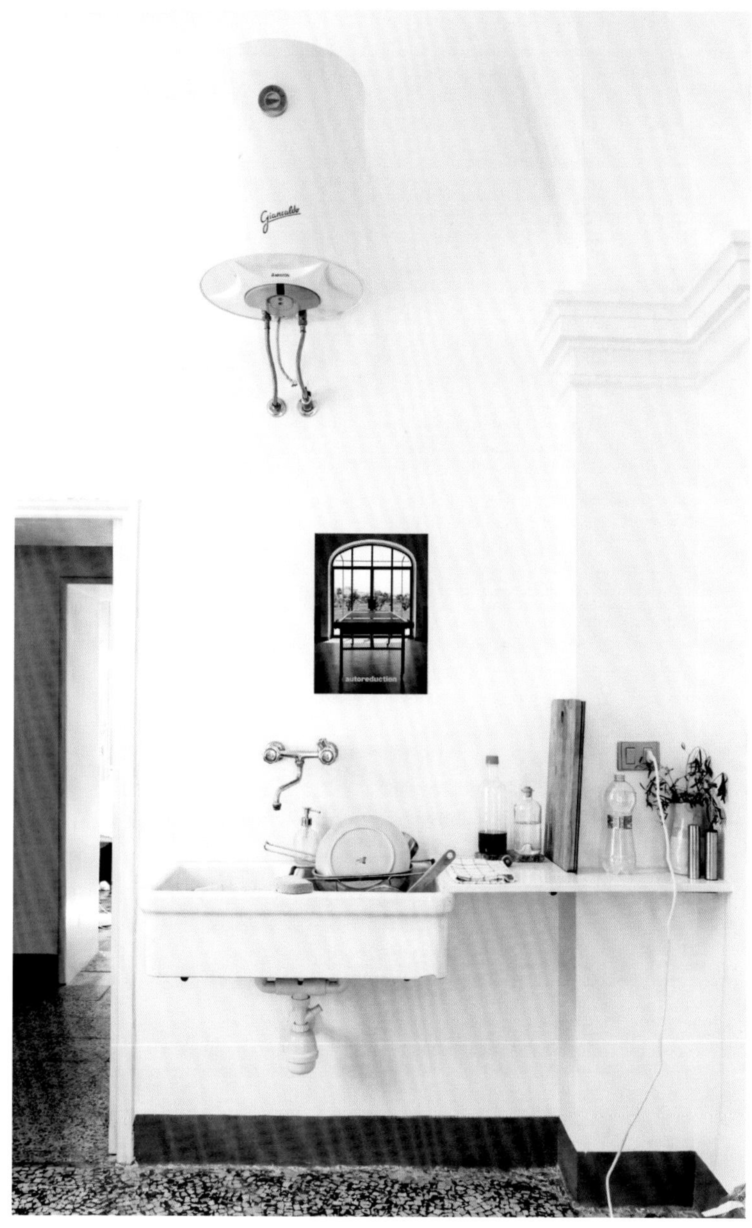
autoreduction

This book has been published by Progetto, Lecce; Oaza, Zagreb; and Mousse Publishing, Milan in conjunction with the exhibition:

Dora Budor
Autoreduction
With Noah Barker, Niloufar Emamifar, Michèle Graf and Selina Grüter, and Ser Serpas

Progetto, Lecce, Italy
July 16–September 30, 2021

Book
Editor—Dora Budor
Publishing Editor—Antonio Scoccimarro (Mousse Publishing)
Texts—Marina Vishmidt, Noah Barker
Copy Editing—Domenick Ammirati
Graphic Design—Nina Bačun, Roberta Bratović (Oaza, Zagreb)
Photography—Simon Veres (pg. 71–111), Alice Caracciolo (pg. 16–23; 106–107).
All other photography by the authors unless otherwise noted.
Cover image—image by Alice Caracciolo; poster by Dora Budor

Published and distributed by
Mousse Publishing
Via Pier Candido Decembrio 28
20137, Milan, Italy
moussemagazine.it

Available through
Mousse Publishing, Milan
moussemagazine.it

DAP | Distributed Art Publishers, New York
artbook.com

Idea Books, Amsterdam
ideabooks.nl

Les presses du réel, Dijon
lespressesdureel.com

First edition: 2022

Printed in Italy by Grafiche Veneziane, Italy
ISBN 9788867495733

€ 22 / $ 25

With the kind support from
Maximilian Hagemes
Leonardo Dal Colle

Special thanks to
Eduardo Andres Alfonso, Lorenzo and Isabell Bertoli, Diego Moretto, Will Sanderson, Stella Berkofsky, Pantaleo Greco, Pietro Luigi Nuccio, Isabella Mongelli, Veronica Centonze, Alessio Cerfeda, Chiara Papaleo, Federico Rizzo, Veronica Vergari, Marco Vitale, Gabriele Calvara, Carmelo De Lorenzis, Simone Mazzeo, Angela Durante, Mario Di Donfrancesco, Cesare Papaleo, and the Papaleo family.